Secrets of Expert Card Play

David Bird and Tony Forrester

B.T. Batsford Ltd, *London*

First published 1997

© David Bird and Tony Forrester 1997

ISBN 0 7134 8281 8

Typeset by Apsbridge Services Ltd, Nottingham.
Printed by Redwood Books, Trowbridge, Wiltshire
for the publishers,
B. T. Batsford Ltd, 583 Fulham Road,
London SW6 5BY

A BATSFORD BRIDGE BOOK

Series Editor: Tony Sowter
Commissioning Editor: Paul Lamford

CONTENTS

1
PUTTING TRUMPS TO WORK

Jumping straight in at the deep end, we begin by looking at how you can retain control of a hand when the trump suit is fragile. Tony arrived in a 5-2 trump fit on this deal from the 1996 Marchessini tournament at the Portland Club.

Love All. Dealer South.

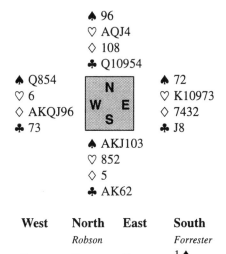

	♠ 96	
	♡ AQJ4	
	◇ 108	
	♣ Q10954	

♠ Q854		♠ 72
♡ 6		♡ K10973
◇ AKQJ96		◇ 7432
♣ 73		♣ J8

	♠ AKJ103	
	♡ 852	
	◇ 5	
	♣ AK62	

West	North	East	South
	Robson		*Forrester*
–	–	–	1♠
2◇	Dble	3◇	3♠
Pass	4♠	All Pass	

North's double was for take-out (a negative double). Although a club fit was likely, it was natural for South to seek a cheaper game in his sturdy major suit. Suppose you had been declarer in Four Spades. How would you have reacted when West began with two top diamonds?

On some hands it would work well to discard on the second round of diamonds. You could then ruff a diamond continuation in the dummy, preserving your five-card trump holding. Such an approach would be dangerous here since a heart switch would be unwelcome.

Tony followed a different path. He ruffed the second diamond, then led the 10 of trumps from hand! Do you see the point of this play? Declarer can afford to lose a trump trick. By conceding this loser on the first round of trumps, he prevents a further attack on his trump length. If West wins with the queen and plays a third round of diamonds, the force can be taken in the dummy. Whether or not West continues his attack in diamonds, declarer has no intention of taking a finesse in hearts. After winning West's return and drawing trumps, he can score ten tricks simply by running the club suit.

Sometimes it is not your trump length which is under threat but your trump honours. You may need to play the trump suit in an unusual way to prevent the defenders establishing an extra trump trick. Look at this deal:

East/West Game. Dealer South.

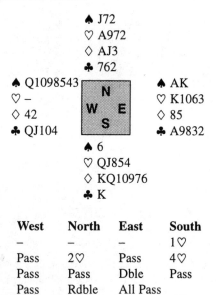

```
                    ♠ J72
                    ♡ A972
                    ◇ AJ3
                    ♣ 762
    ♠ Q1098543                  ♠ AK
    ♡ –           N            ♡ K1063
    ◇ 42        W   E          ◇ 85
    ♣ QJ104        S           ♣ A9832
                    ♠ 6
                    ♡ QJ854
                    ◇ KQ10976
                    ♣ K
```

West	North	East	South
–	–	–	1♡
Pass	2♡	Pass	4♡
Pass	Pass	Dble	Pass
Pass	Rdble	All Pass	

Perhaps West didn't notice that he held seven spades! North certainly have regretted his redouble, had West emerged from his slumbers and removed to Four Spades. The defenders led clubs against Four Hearts, declarer ruffing the second round. Giving the hand insufficient attention, he continued with ace and another trump. When East rose with the king and played another club, South had to ruff with an honour. East's ♡10 became the setting trick. Do you see how declarer can do better?

The answer is to run the queen of trumps instead of playing ace and another. Suppose East wins with the trump king and plays two top spades, reducing South's trumps to J8. Declarer can cross to dummy with a diamond, finesse the 8 of trumps, and cash the trump jack. He then returns to dummy with a diamond and draws East's last trump, claiming the balance.

On the next deal Australian international, Tim Bourke, employed a different technique for retaining control – running a powerful side suit.

North/South Game. Dealer North.

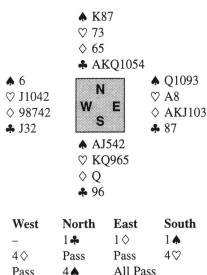

```
                    ♠ K87
                    ♡ 73
                    ◊ 65
                    ♣ AKQ1054
    ♠ 6                              ♠ Q1093
    ♡ J1042          N               ♡ A8
    ◊ 98742      W       E           ◊ AKJ103
    ♣ J32            S               ♣ 87
                    ♠ AJ542
                    ♡ KQ965
                    ◊ Q
                    ♣ 96
```

West	North	East	South
–	1♣	1◊	1♠
4◊	Pass	Pass	4♡
Pass	4♠	All Pass	

Over the 1◊ overcall some South players would say 'I have both the unbid suits, I'll start with a negative double'. That's not a good idea when you hold 5-card suits, since you don't need 4-card support to make a playable fit. If South starts with a negative double on this deal, he would have little option but to double again when 4◊ comes back to him. +100 for one down would be lean pickings.

Diamonds were led against Four Spades and Bourke ruffed the second round. Suppose declarer crosses to the trump king next and finesses the jack of trumps. When West shows out there will be no way to make the contract. The Australian found a stronger line. He crossed to the ace of clubs and finessed the trump jack. West showed out when the ace of trumps was played, but the 4-1 break now posed no problem. Declarer could run dummy's clubs until East ruffed. Back in control, he could then ruff the diamond continuation and cross to the trump king to enjoy the remaining clubs. Five tricks in each black suit would land the game.

Even when your trump suit is as handsome as AKQJxx, there may be a risk of losing control. It happened to an unwary declarer on this deal:

East/West Game. Dealer South.

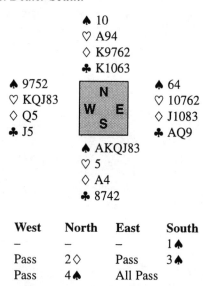

                        ♠ 10
                        ♡ A94
                        ◊ K9762
                        ♣ K1063
        ♠ 9752   ♠ 64
        ♡ KQJ83   N   ♡ 10762
        ◊ Q5   W   E   ◊ J1083
        ♣ J5   S   ♣ AQ9
                        ♠ AKQJ83
                        ♡ 5
                        ◊ A4
                        ♣ 8742

West	North	East	South
–	–	–	1♠
Pass	2◊	Pass	3♠
Pass	4♠	All Pass	

Quite right, 3NT would have been better! However, South's struggles in Four Spades may prove instructive. He won the king of hearts lead and drew trumps in four rounds. A club to the 10 lost to the queen and East forced South with a heart. Declarer led a second round of clubs to the jack, king and ace. A third round of hearts removed his last trump and that was one down. Declarer did not score a trick from the club suit.

Let's have another go. Suppose that you start on the side suit at trick 2, leading a low club from dummy. Many Easts will make life easy for you, going in with the queen. We'll assume that this particular East is a superior character and plays the 9. The defenders win the trick and force you with a heart. You lead a second round of clubs to the king, East winning with the ace and forcing you again in hearts. Unperturbed, you clear the club suit. A fourth round of hearts does no damage now. You will be able to ruff in the dummy! As soon as you regain the lead you will draw trumps and claim the balance.

Preventing enemy ruffs

Let's move to something different – how to avoid enemy ruffs. Several declarers misplayed the following deal when it arose in a simultaneous pairs.

East/West Game. Dealer South.

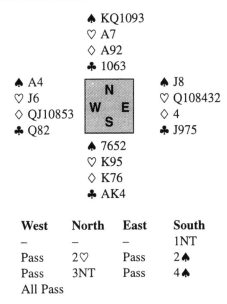

```
                  ♠ KQ1093
                  ♡ A7
                  ◇ A92
                  ♣ 1063
   ♠ A4            ┌─────────┐      ♠ J8
   ♡ J6            │   N     │      ♡ Q108432
   ◇ QJ10853       │ W   E   │      ◇ 4
   ♣ Q82           │   S     │      ♣ J975
                   └─────────┘
                  ♠ 7652
                  ♡ K95
                  ◇ K76
                  ♣ AK4
```

West	North	East	South
–	–	–	1NT
Pass	2♡	Pass	2♠
Pass	3NT	Pass	4♠
All Pass			

South arrived in Four Spades after a transfer sequence and West led the queen of diamonds. The unsuspecting declarers won with the king and led a trump towards dummy. Not the best! The various Wests had noted their partners' ◇ 4 at trick 1. They rose, as one, with the ace and played the jack of diamonds. East ruffed dummy's diamond ace and the contract was now under threat. After drawing trumps and eliminating the heart suit, declarer had to try three rounds of clubs, hoping that East would win and have to give a ruff-and-discard. No such luck. West won the third round with the queen and that was one down.

The mistake came at trick 1. If diamonds were 6-1 it was very likely that West held the six, rather than a singleton queen. Declarer should have won the first trick with dummy's ace. He could then cross to the king of hearts (choosing the shortest side suit) to play a trump. After such a start no damage would be done if West rose with the ace and returned a diamond. East would be welcome to ruff a loser.

Many a damaging ruff can be averted, simply by leading towards your honour cards. On this deal the focus is on the diamond suit:

North/South Game. Dealer South.

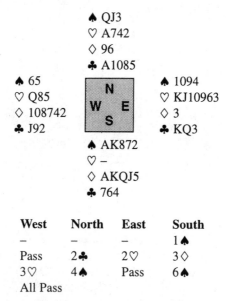

```
                    ♠ QJ3
                    ♡ A742
                    ◇ 96
                    ♣ A1085
   ♠ 65            ┌─────────┐         ♠ 1094
   ♡ Q85           │   N     │         ♡ KJ10963
   ◇ 108742        │ W   E   │         ◇ 3
   ♣ J92           │   S     │         ♣ KQ3
                    └─────────┘
                    ♠ AK872
                    ♡ –
                    ◇ AKQJ5
                    ♣ 764
```

West	North	East	South
–	–	–	1♠
Pass	2♣	2♡	3◇
3♡	4♠	Pass	6♠
All Pass			

West leads ♡5 against Six Spades and you win with dummy's ace, discarding a club. If the diamonds are no worse than 4-2 there will be twelve tricks on top. What can be done if the diamonds break 5-1 or 6-0? One possibility is to draw just two rounds of trumps with the ace and queen, then play on diamonds. If the defender with the long diamonds also holds the last trump, the two high diamonds will stand up and it will be possible to ruff a diamond.

That line would not be good enough on the layout shown; East would ruff the second diamond. This ruff can be avoided, however, by leading the first two rounds of diamonds towards the South hand. At trick two you play a diamond towards the ace. You then return to dummy with the queen of trumps to lead a second diamond. It will do East no good to ruff a loser; you would then be able to discard three of dummy's clubs on your good diamonds, eventually ruffing a club in dummy. Nor can East defeat you by discarding on the second diamond. After winning with the king, you would ruff a diamond high and return to hand with a heart. You could then draw trumps and claim twelve tricks.

A final technique in the war against adverse ruffs is to discard the card which might be ruffed. Declarer played carelessly when this deal arose:

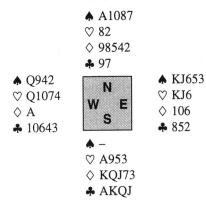

```
                    ♠ A1087
                    ♡ 82
                    ◇ 98542
                    ♣ 97
    ♠ Q942            N         ♠ KJ653
    ♡ Q1074                     ♡ KJ6
    ◇ A          W       E      ◇ 106
    ♣ 10643           S         ♣ 852
                    ♠ –
                    ♡ A953
                    ◇ KQJ73
                    ♣ AKQJ
```

South arrived in Six Diamonds and West found the awkward lead of a heart. Declarer won with the ace and had to dispose of dummy's losing heart before playing on trumps. Three rounds of clubs stood up, he was pleased to see, and away went dummy's heart loser. When trumps were played West won with the ace and cruelly played a fourth round of clubs. East ruffed with the 10 of trumps and that was one down.

Declarer's last club was an embarrassment to him. Before playing on trumps he should have reached dummy with a heart ruff and discarded his last club honour on the ace of spades.

Establishing a side suit

When dummy has a side suit such as AKxxx, the prospect of establishing extra tricks by setting up the suit is obvious. Less glamorous holdings may prove productive too. Tony sat South on this deal from the final of the 1979 Hubert Phillips Bowl (which his team lost by just 60 aggregate points).

Love All. Dealer South.

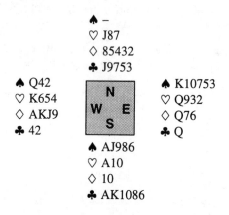

	♠ –	
	♡ J87	
	◇ 85432	
	♣ J9753	
♠ Q42		♠ K10753
♡ K654		♡ Q932
◇ AKJ9		◇ Q76
♣ 42		♣ Q
	♠ AJ986	
	♡ A10	
	◇ 10	
	♣ AK1086	

West	North	East	South
	Oldroyd		*Forrester*
–	–	–	1♠
Dble	Pass	2♡	3♣
Pass	4♣	Pass	5♣
Pass	Pass	Dble	All Pass

West led a trump against Tony's Five Clubs doubled and the queen was taken by South's ace. It may seem attractive to start ruffing spades at this point. But the spades are unlikely to be 4-4 after West's take-out double and when West gains the lead in diamonds he will play a second trump. Tony's eye was drawn to dummy's diamond suit. If diamonds were to break 4-3 an extra trick could be established there.

At trick 2 Tony played a diamond. West won and returned a second trump, won in the dummy. There was now time to set up a long diamond. Declarer scored five trumps in his hand, three spade ruffs, the major-suit aces and a long diamond.

When you have the chance of establishing a side suit for discards it may pay you to make the second-best play in the trump suit. Suppose this is your trump suit:

♠ KJ74

♠ A632

Looking at the suit in isolation, the best play is to cash the ace, then finesse the jack. However, if the opening lead has exposed you to some losers elsewhere, you may prefer to cash the ace and king of trumps. This will annoy East if he holds Qx. And if the queen does not fall, you may be able to attend to your losers.

The technique was used successfully on this deal:

Love All. Dealer North.

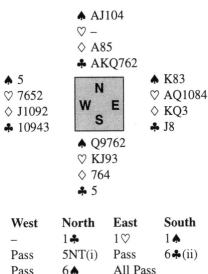

```
              ♠ AJ104
              ♡ –
              ◊ A85
              ♣ AKQ762
♠ 5                          ♠ K83
♡ 7652          N            ♡ AQ1084
◊ J1092      W     E         ◊ KQ3
♣ 10943         S            ♣ J8
              ♠ Q9762
              ♡ KJ93
              ◊ 764
              ♣ 5
```

West	North	East	South
–	1♣	1♡	1♠
Pass	5NT(i)	Pass	6♣(ii)
Pass	6♠	All Pass	

(i) Grand Slam force
(ii) One top trump honour

It was clear from North's bidding that a heart lead would be unproductive. West led the jack of diamonds and the slam was now in danger. West might well have held the trump king and if declarer wanted to finesse in trumps he could reach his hand with a club ruff. However, with the diamond suit exposed, a failing trump finesse would lead to immediate defeat. Declarer preferred to cash the ace of trumps. When the king failed to appear, he turned to the club suit. All followed to the ace and king, and one diamond was discarded. The queen of clubs was now led.

If East were to ruff high, or to discard, declarer would dispose of his last diamond and score twelve tricks easily. At the table East chose to ruff low. Declarer overruffed, returned to dummy with a heart ruff, and ruffed the club suit good. He then returned to dummy with a second heart ruff and led a master club. It was the end of the road for East. Whether or not he ruffed with the trump king, declarer's losing diamond would go away.

Declarer's line of play would have succeeded also if clubs were 3-3, or if the defender with only two clubs had to ruff with the trump king. The combination of all these chances was greater than that of a simple trump finesse.

The cross-ruff

When both hands contain a shortage, the best play may be to score the trumps in the two hands separately: the familiar cross-ruff. It is a form of play which contains some pitfalls.

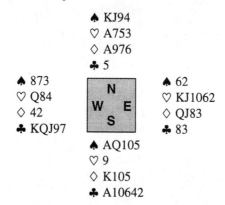

You climb to Six Spades and West leads the king of clubs. After winning with the ace, how should you continue?

There are four top winners outside the trump suit. If you can score all eight of your trumps separately, ruffing clubs and hearts in turn, you will bring your total to the magic 12. The first point to note is that you should cash two diamond tricks immediately. Otherwise the defenders may be able to discard diamonds during the cross-ruff and you will never score the two winners. The other point is that the early ruffs (two in this case) should be made with small trumps, at which time you hope the defenders will have to follow suit.

A cross-ruff sometimes ends with the promotion of a bare trump honour. That's what happened on this deal:

East/West Game. Dealer South.

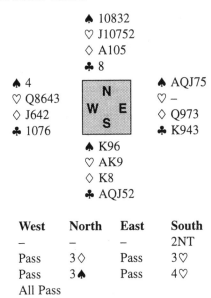

	♠ 10832	
	♡ J10752	
	◇ A105	
	♣ 8	

West		East
♠ 4		♠ AQJ75
♡ Q8643		♡ –
◇ J642		◇ Q973
♣ 1076		♣ K943

	♠ K96	
	♡ AK9	
	◇ K8	
	♣ AQJ52	

West	North	East	South
–	–	–	2NT
Pass	3◇	Pass	3♡
Pass	3♠	Pass	4♡
All Pass			

South ended in Four Hearts after a transfer sequence and West led his singleton spade. East won with the ace and returned the spade queen, covered by the king and ruffed by West. Back came ◇ 2, East's 9 drawing South's king. The contract assumed some difficulty when East showed out on the ace of trumps. Declarer's first task was to read the club suit. Who was likely to hold the club king? If West's diamond 2 was a true fourth-best his shape would be 1-5-4-3, making East a 4-3 favourite to hold ♣ K.

Declarer crossed to the diamond ace and finessed the queen of clubs successfully. He then discarded a spade on the ace of clubs, ruffed a club, and ruffed a diamond with the 9. The lead was in the South hand in this end position:

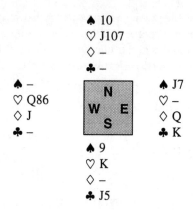

♠ 10
♡ J107
◇ –
♣ –

♠ –
♡ Q86
◇ J
♣ –

♠ J7
♡ –
◇ Q
♣ K

♠ 9
♡ K
◇ –
♣ J5

What could West do when a club was played? If he ruffed high, declarer would throw a spade from dummy, claiming the last three tricks with high trumps. West postponed his fate by discarding the diamond jack. Declarer ruffed the club in dummy, returned to his hand with a trump to the king, and led the last club. This promoted dummy's bare jack of trumps and brought the total to ten tricks: two diamonds, two clubs, and six tricks from the trump suit.

Tony used the same style of play on a deal from the 1985 Swiss Teams Congress in Leeds, an event which Forrester/Brock and Kirby/Armstrong went on to win.

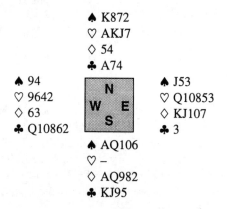

♠ K872
♡ AKJ7
◇ 54
♣ A74

♠ 94
♡ 9642
◇ 63
♣ Q10862

♠ J53
♡ Q10853
◇ KJ107
♣ 3

♠ AQ106
♡ –
◇ AQ982
♣ KJ95

Tony arrived in Six Spades and West led ♡6, covered by the jack and queen and ruffed in the South hand. After a club to the ace, the queen of diamonds was finessed successfully. Both defenders followed to the ace and queen of trumps. Tony now cashed the diamond ace and ruffed a third round of diamonds, West showing out. The best prospect at this stage was to switch to a cross-ruff. If declarer could score six side-suit winners to accompany his two tricks in the trump suit, he could bring his total to twelve by scoring the last four trumps separately.

Tony cashed dummy's two heart winners, discarding a club and a diamond. These cards remained:

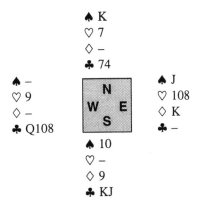

When a club was led from dummy East could not gain by ruffing a loser. He discarded a heart and declarer scored the king of clubs. Now came a diamond ruff with the king and a heart from the table. East could not prevent the promotion of South's ♠ 10, *en passant*, and that was twelve tricks.

The dummy reversal

We'll end this first chapter with a look at an old friend – the dummy reversal. Suppose you are in Four Spades with this trump suit:

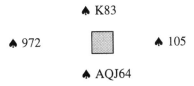

You start with five trump tricks. If you can score a ruff in the North hand, with the short trump holding, you will turn five into six. Taking a ruff in the long trump hand would not add directly to your trick total; you would still have only five trump tricks. But what if you could take *three* ruffs in the South hand? Again the total would climb to six.

That's the idea of a dummy reversal. You ruff in declarer's hand, normally the longer trump holding, pretending for a moment that it is the dummy. Here is an example from a 1983 Crockford's semi-final:

North/South Game. Dealer South.

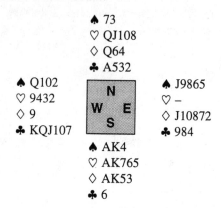

♠ 73
♡ QJ108
◇ Q64
♣ A532

♠ Q102   ♠ J9865
♡ 9432   ♡ –
◇ 9   ◇ J10872
♣ KQJ107   ♣ 984

♠ AK4
♡ AK765
◇ AK53
♣ 6

West	North	East	South
	Brock		*Forrester*
–	–	–	1♡
Pass	3♡	Pass	4NT
Pass	5◇	Pass	5♠
Pass	5NT	Pass	7♡
All Pass			

South's 4NT was Roman Key-Card Blackwood. The 5♠ follow-up asked for the trump queen and the 5NT response showed that card but denied any side-suit king. Tony won the king of clubs lead with the ace. There were only six top cards outside the trump suit, so unless diamonds were 3-3 he would need to score seven trump tricks. Taking two ruffs in the dummy would require a 2-2 trump break, or the defender with the long trump to hold four diamonds.

Tony surveyed the hand again, this time from the North seat. It seemed it would be easier to ruff three clubs in the South hand. He ruffed a club at trick 2 and led a trump to the queen, East showing out. The rest of the play was easy: club ruff with the ace, trump to the 8, club ruff with the king. Tony could now draw trumps and claim the slam.

Count the tricks that were made. Six side-suit winners, four trumps in dummy and three ruffs in hand. Many players have a mental block with regard to dummy reversals. When you arrive in a trump contract, make a habit of surveying prospects from both sides of the table.

A dummy reversal was the answer on the next hand too, played by Tony in the 1980 Olympiad. The opponents were Sweden and at the other table Flodqvist and Sundelin had stopped in a modest Four Spades.

North/South Game. Dealer East.

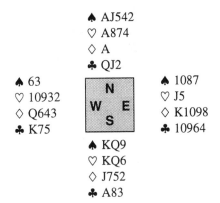

```
                    ♠ AJ542
                    ♡ A874
                    ◇ A
                    ♣ QJ2
   ♠ 63                          ♠ 1087
   ♡ 10932          N            ♡ J5
   ◇ Q643      W         E       ◇ K1098
   ♣ K75             S           ♣ 10964
                    ♠ KQ9
                    ♡ KQ6
                    ◇ J752
                    ♣ A83
```

West	North	East	South
Morath	*Smolski*	*Gothe*	*Forrester*
–	–	Pass	1NT
Pass	2♡	Pass	2♠
Pass	3♡	Pass	4♠
Pass	6♠	All Pass	

Morath made the aggressive lead of a club, dummy's queen winning. Even after this helpful start the route to twelve tricks is unclear if you survey matters from the long-trump hand (North). There is still a club to lose and you must somehow deal with the fourth round of hearts.

Suppose you consider the affair from the South hand instead, attempting to dispose of the losers there. If you can ruff all three diamond losers, you will have only one club loser remaining.

Tony cashed the ace of diamonds at trick 2, played a spade to the king, and ruffed a diamond. He then led the jack of trumps, hoping to see the 10 appear on his right. In that case he could have overtaken with the queen and later re-entered his hand with the trump 9, not needing to risk an adverse ruff elsewhere. When the 10 did not show, Tony let the jack hold. He then played a heart to the queen, ruffed a second diamond, returned to his hand with a heart to the king, and ruffed his last diamond with the ace of trumps. These cards remained:

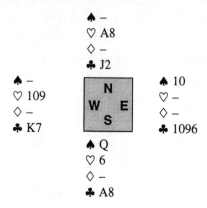

                    ♠ –
                    ♡ A8
                    ◇ –
                    ♣ J2

    ♠ –   ♠ 10
    ♡ 109   N   ♡ –
    ◇ –   W   E   ◇ –
    ♣ K7   S   ♣ 1096

                    ♠ Q
                    ♡ 6
                    ◇ –
                    ♣ A8

A club to the ace allowed the last trump to be drawn. On this trick West was squeezed in hearts and clubs, giving Tony a rather surprising overtrick.

When you are playing in a 4-4 fit, the notion of a dummy reversal is somewhat artificial. Nevertheless, with four trumps in each hand you should make a habit of looking at the play from both sides of the table. That's what Australia's Ian Thomson did on this deal:

North/South Game. Dealer South.

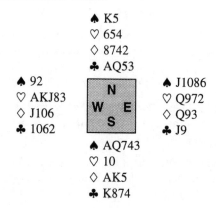

                    ♠ K5
                    ♡ 654
                    ◇ 8742
                    ♣ AQ53

    ♠ 92   ♠ J1086
    ♡ AKJ83   N   ♡ Q972
    ◇ J106   W   E   ◇ Q93
    ♣ 1062   S   ♣ J9

                    ♠ AQ743
                    ♡ 10
                    ◇ AK5
                    ♣ K874

West	North	East	South
–	–	–	1♠
Pass	1NT	Pass	2♣
2♡	3♣	Pass	4♡
Pass	4♠	Pass	5♣
Pass	6♣	All Pass	

West led the king of hearts, East following with the 9 to show an even number of cards in the suit. With nothing further to be drawn from this particular well, West switched to the jack of diamonds, won with the ace.

Suppose you view prospects from the South seat. After drawing trumps, you would need spades to be 3-3. You would then be able to discard two diamonds from dummy and ruff a diamond for your twelfth trick. Do prospects look any better from the North seat? Yes, you could ruff two hearts, then perhaps establish the spades to discard North's diamond losers.

Thomson set off on this path. After winning the diamond switch, he crossed to the ace of clubs and ruffed a heart. He returned to dummy with the spade king and ruffed another heart. Both defenders followed when the bare king of trumps was cashed. Thomson then cashed the ace of spades and led a third round of the suit. When a discard came from West, he ruffed in the dummy, drew West's last trump, and claimed the remainder. There was nothing particularly difficult about it, except having the imagination, or discipline, to rotate the hand through 180 degrees.

Entries to the hand with the shorter trump holding can be critical. This slam hand was misplayed at several tables when it arose in a pairs tournament in Paris:

Love All. Dealer East.

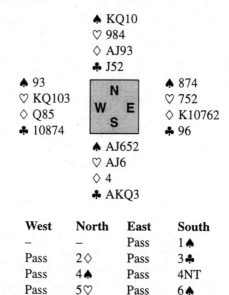

♠ KQ10
♡ 984
◇ AJ93
♣ J52

♠ 93
♡ KQ103
◇ Q85
♣ 10874

♠ 874
♡ 752
◇ K10762
♣ 96

♠ AJ652
♡ AJ6
◇ 4
♣ AKQ3

West	North	East	South
–	–	Pass	1♠
Pass	2◇	Pass	3♣
Pass	4♠	Pass	4NT
Pass	5♡	Pass	6♠
All Pass			

South arrived in Six Spades, West leading the king of hearts. Hoping for a heart continuation into the ace-jack, several Souths contributed ♡6 to the first trick (a Bath Coup). Do you see why this is a poor idea?

A heart continuation is most unlikely, particularly when East has played a discouraging 2 at trick 1 and the bidding marks South with a control in hearts. Declarer should consider how else the contract might be made. If trumps are 3-2 he will be able to ruff three diamonds in the South hand, draw trumps with North's holding, then discard one of dummy's hearts on the fourth round of clubs. The sequence of play will be: ace of diamonds, diamond ruff low, jack of clubs, diamond ruffed with the jack, trump to the king, diamond ruffed with the ace. Then a trump to the queen allows you to draw the last trump with the 10.

If instead you duck the heart lead and West switches to a trump, which is surely the likely continuation, you will be one entry short!

2
ELIMINATION PLAY

Has it ever occurred to you that it is never an advantage to be the first to play on a particular suit? If the opponents start the suit instead, you will never be worse off and will often score an extra trick. Look at these typical holdings:

(a) Q63

J54

(b) A42

J103

(c) A72

Q63

You might make a trick under your own steam on (a); if the opponents are first to play the suit, that trick is a certainty. In position (b) you have poor chances of two tricks if you play the suit yourself (you would need to find a singleton honour or a chosen defender with a doubleton honour). If the defenders play the suit, you will have a clear-cut finesse on the second round. In (c) you will make two tricks roughly half the time. If you can arrange for West to lead the suit a second trick is certain.

We're agreed, then. You would like the defenders to open your key suit. How can you arrange it? The most common method, and one of the most important techniques in a trump contract, is known as 'elimination play'. You eliminate one or more side suits, so that the defenders cannot play on those without conceding a ruff-and-discard, then throw a defender on lead.

This is a typical example, featuring the heart holding in (b) above:

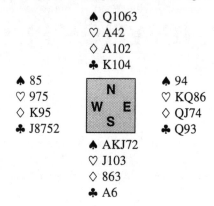

♠ Q1063
♡ A42
◇ A102
♣ K104

♠ 85   ♠ 94
♡ 975   ♡ KQ86
◇ K95   ◇ QJ74
♣ J8752   ♣ Q93

♠ AKJ72
♡ J103
◇ 863
♣ A6

South arrives in Four Spades. A heart lead would have worked well but West starts with a trump. Declarer draws trumps with the ace and king, then plays a diamond, inserting dummy's 10. East wins and exits safely in one or other minor. Declarer eliminates the club suit (by cashing two rounds and ruffing the third), then cuts loose by playing ace and another diamond. The next move is the opponents' and they are welcome to it. This is the position:

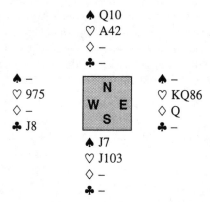

♠ Q10
♡ A42
◇ –
♣ –

♠ –   ♠ –
♡ 975   ♡ KQ86
◇ –   ◇ Q
♣ J8   ♣ –

♠ J7
♡ J103
◇ –
♣ –

It makes no difference on this particular hand which defender is on lead. If a club or diamond is led, declarer will ruff in one hand, discard a heart from the other. If instead either defender leads a heart, declarer will lose only one trick there (a low heart from West will be passed to East, who will then be end-played).

Note declarer's play of a diamond to the 10, which forced the safe (East) hand to win. Had he carelessly played the ace and 2 of diamonds, West could have won the second round with the 9. A heart through, followed by a diamond to the king and another heart, would have beaten the contract.

Elimination hands occur time and time again. Sometimes you even exit in the key suit itself:

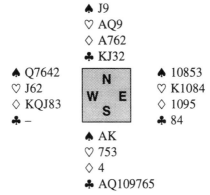

```
                      ♠ J9
                      ♡ AQ9
                      ◊ A762
                      ♣ KJ32
    ♠ Q7642                        ♠ 10853
    ♡ J62           N              ♡ K1084
    ◊ KQJ83      W     E           ◊ 1095
    ♣ –             S              ♣ 84
                      ♠ AK
                      ♡ 753
                      ◊ 4
                      ♣ AQ109765
```

You reach 6♣ and West leads the ◊ K. The key suit is clearly hearts, where you hope to avoid two losers. Think as follows: 'I'm going to draw trumps, eliminate spades and diamonds, then play a heart to the 9, end-playing East'.

Entries to the dummy are not plentiful. Once you plan the hand in detail you will see that you must start to eliminate diamonds immediately, before drawing any trumps. After winning the diamond lead with the ace, you ruff a diamond high. You then cross to the king of trumps and ruff another diamond high. A trump to the jack draws East's last trump and allows you to ruff dummy's last diamond. You cash the ace and king of spades, arriving at the desired end position:

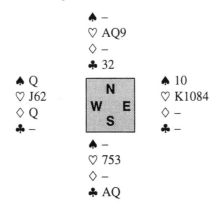

```
                      ♠ –
                      ♡ AQ9
                      ◊ –
                      ♣ 32
    ♠ Q                            ♠ 10
    ♡ J62           N              ♡ K1084
    ◊ Q           W     E          ◊ –
    ♣ –             S              ♣ –
                      ♠ –
                      ♡ 753
                      ◊ –
                      ♣ AQ
```

A heart to the 9 leaves East end-played, forced to concede a ruff-and-discard or to lead a heart into the tenace. It would not help West to insert the jack on the first round of hearts; this would be covered by the queen and king, and East would have to lead into dummy's ♡A9.

These have been relatively straightforward examples of the technique. Sometimes you will have to read the cards well to decide on the best line. Here declarer makes use of the fact that West has opened the bidding:

Game All. Dealer West.

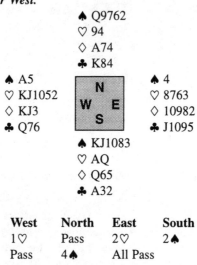

```
                    ♠ Q9762
                    ♡ 94
                    ◇ A74
                    ♣ K84
    ♠ A5               N            ♠ 4
    ♡ KJ1052      W       E        ♡ 8763
    ◇ KJ3             S            ◇ 10982
    ♣ Q76                          ♣ J1095
                    ♠ KJ1083
                    ♡ AQ
                    ◇ Q65
                    ♣ A32
```

West	North	East	South
1♡	Pass	2♡	2♠
Pass	4♠	All Pass	

A heart lead would have been welcome but West starts warily with ace and another trump. Declarer's first move is to play ace, king and another club. Should West win the third round, the contract will be secure; he will have to open one of the red suits. West spots the danger and drops the queen of clubs under your ace. East now wins the third round of clubs and switches to a heart. In the absence of any bidding you would have to guess whether to finesse the heart queen. After West's opening bid, however, it is a near certainty that the heart king is offside. You rise with the ace of hearts and exit with the heart queen. West is on lead and must now lead from the king of diamonds or concede a ruff-and-discard.

To prepare for an elimination it may be necessary to cash a round or two of the key suit. Suppose you are blessed with this side suit:

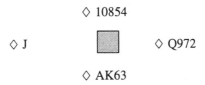

◇ 10854

◇ J   ◇ Q972

◇ AK63

Once you have cashed the ace and king, neither defender can safely play a diamond.

Such preparation was done for the declarer on this deal from a Crockford's match:

North/South Game. Dealer South.

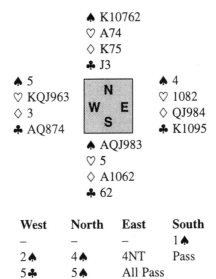

♠ K10762
♡ A74
◇ K75
♣ J3

♠ 5
♡ KQJ963
◇ 3
♣ AQ874

♠ 4
♡ 1082
◇ QJ984
♣ K1095

♠ AQJ983
♡ 5
◇ A1062
♣ 62

West	North	East	South
–	–	–	1♠
2♠	4♠	4NT	Pass
5♣	5♠	All Pass	

West's ♠2 overcall was a Michaels cue-bid, showing hearts and one of the minors. East's 4NT asked for partner's minor and North's decision to press on to the five level was borderline at best. What would you have led from the West hand? The original West made the poor choice of his singleton diamond. Declarer won East's jack with the ace, drew trumps, and eliminated the heart suit. When he exited in clubs there was nothing the defenders could do. Whoever won the second round of clubs would be end-played.

West's diamond lead was likely to succeed only when East held the diamond ace. In that case West could have afforded to cash the ace of clubs first, awaiting a signal from his partner. East would in fact have encouraged a club continuation. The defenders could then have cashed a second club trick, eventually scoring the setting trick in diamonds.

The play is most interesting on a heart lead. Declarer draws trumps, eliminates hearts, and leads a diamond from dummy. If East splits his honours, he will regret it! Declarer will win with the ace and exit in clubs as before, making the contract. If instead East steels himself to play low, declarer may well rise with the ace, a play which would succeed if West's singleton diamond were an honour.

The next hand was played by Tony in the 1992 Spingold quarter-finals in Washington DC. Success depended on keeping an open mind with regard to West's lead.

East/West Game. Dealer South.

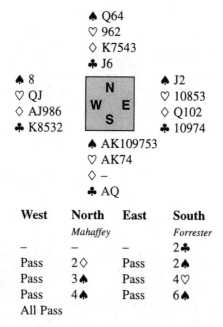

	♠ Q64	
	♡ 962	
	◇ K7543	
	♣ J6	
♠ 8		♠ J2
♡ QJ		♡ 10853
◇ AJ986		◇ Q102
♣ K8532		♣ 10974
	♠ AK109753	
	♡ AK74	
	◇ —	
	♣ AQ	

West	North	East	South
	Mahaffey		*Forrester*
–	–	–	2♣
Pass	2◇	Pass	2♠
Pass	3♠	Pass	4♡
Pass	4♠	Pass	6♠
All Pass			

When West led ♡Q it was a fair initial assumption that he held three or more hearts headed by the QJ or QJ10. Tony won with the king and cashed the ace of trumps, both defenders following.

If the heart suit divided 3-3 it would be possible to discard a club on the fourth heart and then ruff a club. (If the suit lay QJx opposite 10xx, it would be advantageous to duck the second round to West, to prevent East playing a club through before the heart distribution was known.) There were other possibilities in the heart suit, however. Tony drew a second round of trumps with the king, then led a low heart towards the 9. As the cards lay, West won with the bare jack and was end-played, forced to concede a twelfth trick in one of the minors.

Another chance was that West held ♡QJ103, and East ♡85. Again West would be end-played after winning the second heart. Had no luck come from the heart suit, the club finesse would be the final chance.

Exiting in the trump suit

When you plan to exit to a master trump held by a defender, you must be careful that he cannot ruff in prematurely. Tony played this deal in a 1996 Premier League match.

North/South Game. Dealer West.

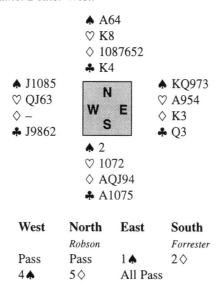

```
                 ♠ A64
                 ♡ K8
                 ◊ 1087652
                 ♣ K4
   ♠ J1085                        ♠ KQ973
   ♡ QJ63          N              ♡ A954
   ◊ –          W     E           ◊ K3
   ♣ J9862         S              ♣ Q3
                 ♠ 2
                 ♡ 1072
                 ◊ AQJ94
                 ♣ A1075
```

West	North	East	South
	Robson		*Forrester*
Pass	Pass	1♠	2◊
4♠	5◊	All Pass	

The jack of spades lead was won in the dummy. Looking at the trump suit in isolation, declarer would finesse the queen. East's opening bid makes him favourite to hold any missing high honour; also, West's jump to Four

Spades on relatively few high cards suggests a marked shortage somewhere. However, a losing trump finesse would lead to certain defeat and there were elimination chances should declarer cash the trump ace and see West show out.

At trick 2 Tony ruffed a spade in the South hand. He then cashed the ace of trumps, West discarding a spade. A club to the king allowed dummy's last spade to be ruffed and declarer continued with the ace of clubs and a club ruff. East refused to overruff but was thrown in with the trump king on the next trick and had to concede the contract.

You may think there was little to the play, but suppose declarer had omitted the spade ruff at trick 2, playing a trump to the ace instead. He would then have to cross to the club king to take the first spade ruff, cash the ace of clubs, and enter dummy via a club ruff to deal with the remaining spade. Disaster! East would overruff with the king and safely play a spade. No elimination and no contract.

One of the most spectacular hands of the 1991 European Championship was an elimination that required a particular lie of the cards:

East/West Game. Dealer East.

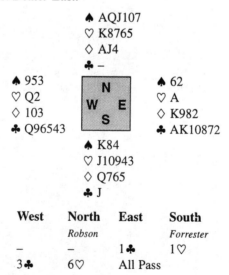

```
              ♠ AQJ107
              ♡ K8765
              ◇ AJ4
              ♣ —
  ♠ 953                    ♠ 62
  ♡ Q2        N            ♡ A
  ◇ 103     W   E          ◇ K982
  ♣ Q96543    S            ♣ AK10872
              ♠ K84
              ♡ J10943
              ◇ Q765
              ♣ J
```

West	North	East	South
	Robson		*Forrester*
–	–	1♣	1♡
3♣	6♡	All Pass	

A lesser man would have been alarmed by North's raise. West led a spade, giving the contract a chance, and Tony won with dummy's 7. The aim now was to end-play East with the bare ace of trumps, having first made sure that he could not exit safely in one of the black suits. Tony played a second round of spades to the king, extracting East's last spade, then ruffed the jack of clubs in dummy. He now called for a low trump. Poor East was on lead and had to surrender the contract!

Loser-on-loser elimination

When you need to throw the lead to one particular defender (because the other defender would have a safe exit card), a special technique may be necessary. It is known as the 'loser-on-loser elimination'. Suppose the key suit is one of these holdings:

(a)   ◇ K65

◇ 742

(b)   ♡ AQ4

♡ 653

There's not much point in forcing West to lead the suit, is there? But if East makes the first play, an extra trick will be guaranteed. Look at this deal, featuring the holding in (b):

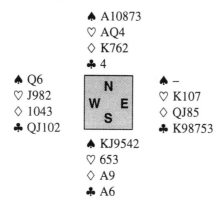

♠ A10873
♡ AQ4
◇ K762
♣ 4

♠ Q6
♡ J982
◇ 1043
♣ QJ102

♠ –
♡ K107
◇ QJ85
♣ K98753

♠ KJ9542
♡ 653
◇ A9
♣ A6

You arrive in Six Spades and West leads the queen of clubs. Suppose you draw trumps, eliminate the minor suits, and lead ♡3. All will be well if West plays a somnolent 2. You will cover with dummy's 4 and leave East end-played. Except in the bottom division of the golf club league, however, West is likely to insert a higher card, such as the 8. Your best chance would then be to duck, hoping that East holds something like ♡K109 and has to overtake. No such luck on this occasion. East would underplay with the 7 and that would be one down.

There is a better way to play the hand. Run the tape back to the point where you ruffed the last of dummy's diamonds. This was the position:

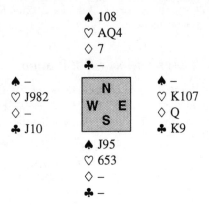

When you lead ◇7 you are pleased to see that it is East who produces the last diamond. Instead of ruffing automatically, throw a heart. This costs nothing, since you were expecting to lose one heart trick anyway. The effect of the play is splendid. East is left on lead and has a choice of ways to commit suicide. You can see why it is called the loser-on-loser elimination. You swap one loser for another, gaining because a particular defender is given the lead.

Tony's very first tournament in partnership with Andy Robson was the 1990 Swiss Teams Congress in Leeds. (Soon afterwards the pair captured two of the world's top invitation events, the Staten Bank and the Sunday Times championships.) This elimination hand arose in the Leeds event:

East/West Game. Dealer West.

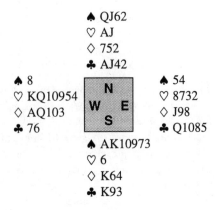

West	North	East	South
	Robson		*Forrester*
1♡	Dble	2♡	4♠
All Pass			

West led the king of hearts, won by dummy's ace. The ace of diamonds was marked offside by the bidding and it might seem that declarer's task was to establish an extra club trick without allowing East, the danger hand, into the lead. Had West held ♣10xx, for example, the contract could have been made by playing a club to the 9.

Tony spotted a stronger line, one that was in fact 100%. After drawing trumps in two rounds, he cashed the king and ace of clubs, then exited with the jack of hearts, throwing the last club from his hand. West could not play either red suit safely and had no clubs in his hand. Ten tricks were guaranteed on any return. West would have been fixed even if he still had one or two clubs in his hand. He could not have played the suit without setting up a winner in dummy.

On the previous example declarer cared little how the cards lay. The contract was secure if West held ♡Q and that was certain after the opening lead. More card-reading was needed on this hand, played by Richard Hyde in the Strang Teams in Glasgow:

Game All. Dealer East.

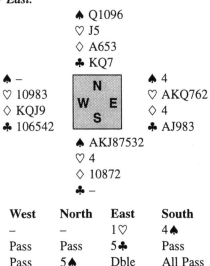

```
                  ♠ Q1096
                  ♡ J5
                  ◊ A653
                  ♣ KQ7
       ♠ —              N            ♠ 4
       ♡ 10983     W       E        ♡ AKQ762
       ◊ KQJ9           S            ◊ 4
       ♣ 106542                      ♣ AJ983
                  ♠ AKJ87532
                  ♡ 4
                  ◊ 10872
                  ♣ —
```

West	North	East	South
–	–	1♡	4♠
Pass	Pass	5♣	Pass
Pass	5♠	Dble	All Pass

West leads the king of diamonds against Five Spades doubled. Dummy's ace wins and East plays the 4. A ruffing finesse in clubs will enable you to dispose of your heart loser. There will still be a risk that diamonds are 4-1 and there are three tricks to be lost in that suit. Knowing how the cards lie, can you see the way out of your predicament?

Hyde won the diamond lead with the ace and called for a low club from dummy. Had East not held the jack of clubs he might have been tempted to rise with the ace, giving declarer two discards. This shot failed, East producing the jack. Declarer ruffed in the South hand and crossed to dummy with a trump. He then led the king of clubs, covered and ruffed. Returning to dummy with another trump, he discarded his heart loser on the club queen and ruffed a heart. Entering the North hand with a third round of trumps, Hyde surveyed this end position:

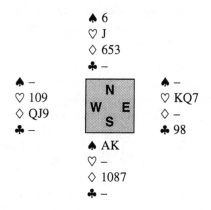

He called for dummy's jack of hearts and, when East covered with the king, threw a diamond from his hand. It was a loser-on-loser elimination. Since East had no diamonds remaining, he was forced to give a ruff-and-discard. Declarer threw another diamond from his hand and ruffed in the dummy. He eventually lost one heart and one diamond, making the contract.

The chosen line would have turned out disastrously, had East held a second diamond. Declarer would have lost one heart and two diamonds, going down when the contract was cold all along. How did he know that diamonds were 4-1, rather than KQJ alone with West and 94 with East? The answer lay in the bidding. If East's shape were 1-5-2-5, West would hold a 0-5-3-5 hand. He would then have corrected to Five Hearts instead of passing Five Clubs.

Partial elimination

For the ruff-and-discard element to be present, you need at least one trump in each hand. Sometimes this means that you cannot draw all the enemy trumps before performing the end-play. Tony sat South on this deal from the 1996 Easter Guardian Pairs.

North/South Game. Dealer South.

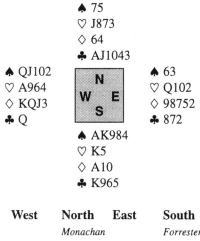

```
                    ♠ 75
                    ♡ J873
                    ◊ 64
                    ♣ AJ1043
    ♠ QJ102                        ♠ 63
    ♡ A964          N              ♡ Q102
    ◊ KQJ3       W     E           ◊ 98752
    ♣ Q             S              ♣ 872
                    ♠ AK984
                    ♡ K5
                    ◊ A10
                    ♣ K965
```

West	North	East	South
	Monachan		*Forrester*
–	–	–	1♠
Pass	1NT	Pass	2♣
Dble	3♣	Pass	5♣
All Pass			

This is not a book on bidding and we do not commend South's final effort to you. 'A typical Forrester overbid' would be a fair description! West led the king of diamonds, won with the ace, and the first problem was how to tackle the trump suit. West's take-out double on the second round suggested he would be short in clubs, so a low club was played towards dummy. The appearance of West's queen carried declarer over the first hurdle.

West's double also marked him with the heart ace, so how could two heart losers be avoided? One chance was to eliminate the spade suit and end-play West with a diamond. Tony cashed the ace and king of spades and ruffed a spade high. He then returned to his hand with a trump and ruffed a fourth round of spades high. This position had been reached:

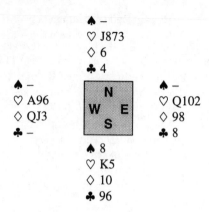

♠ –
♡ J873
◇ 6
♣ 4

♠ –
♡ A96
◇ QJ3
♣ –

♠ –
♡ Q102
◇ 98
♣ 8

♠ 8
♡ K5
◇ 10
♣ 96

The last trump could not be drawn at this stage, since West would then have a safe diamond exit when thrown in. Tony played a diamond immediately. West won and had to concede a ruff-and-discard or lead a heart from the ace. The technique is known as a 'partial elimination' because one or more suits – in this case, trumps – were not completely eliminated.

Despite playing in a 6-5 trump fit, on this deal from the 1991 European Championships, Andy Robson was forced to play a partial elimination.

Game All. Dealer East.

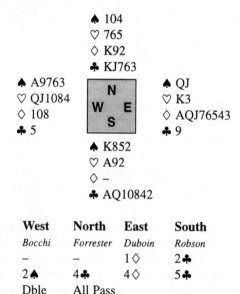

♠ 104
♡ 765
◇ K92
♣ KJ763

♠ A9763
♡ QJ1084
◇ 108
♣ 5

♠ QJ
♡ K3
◇ AQJ76543
♣ 9

♠ K852
♡ A92
◇ –
♣ AQ10842

West	North	East	South
Bocchi	*Forrester*	*Duboin*	*Robson*
–	–	1◇	2♣
2♠	4♣	4◇	5♣
Dble	All Pass		

The British pair at the other table had bid and made Five Diamonds on the East-West cards. So, a healthy 9 IMPs could be written in the plus column if Robson could escape for one down.

The Italian West led the queen of hearts and Robson ducked the trick, anxious to keep East off lead. Hearts were continued and declarer won the second round. The game now was to eliminate West's diamonds and end-play him with a heart. Robson crossed to a trump and ruffed a diamond in the South hand. Returning to dummy with a second round of trumps, he ruffed a second diamond. When Robson exited with a heart West had to win and then had no good return. Whether he played a fourth heart or opened the spades, declarer would lose only one spade trick to go with the two hearts already lost.

It was possible on the bidding that West held a third diamond. So, why did Robson not cross to dummy with a third round of trumps to complete the elimination of the diamond suit? He saw that, if he left himself with only two trumps in the dummy, he would not gain any advantage if West simply played another heart. Restricted to only two spade ruffs, he would lose two spade tricks regardless.

Australia's Roelof Smilde needed to read the cards accurately in our final example of the partial elimination.

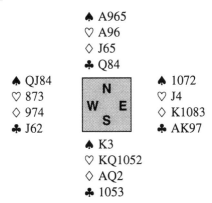

The hand diagram:

                    ♠ A965
                    ♡ A96
                    ◇ J65
                    ♣ Q84
    ♠ QJ84   ♠ 1072
    ♡ 873   N   ♡ J4
    ◇ 974   W   E   ◇ K1083
    ♣ J62   S   ♣ AK97
                    ♠ K3
                    ♡ KQ1052
                    ◇ AQ2
                    ♣ 1053

He arrived in Four Hearts and won the spade queen lead with the king. When the king and ace of trumps were played, East produced the jack on the second round, suggesting that he held only two trumps. Leaving the last enemy trump at large, Smilde finessed ◇Q successfully. He then crossed to the ace of spades and ruffed a spade. The last spade (the jack) clearly lay with West, so, although neither major suit had been completely eliminated, it seemed that East might be ripe for an end-play.

This was the actual position:

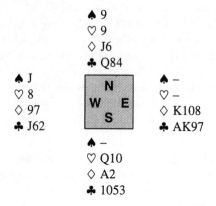

Smilde led a club and coolly inserted dummy's 8. East won with 9, cashed two more club tricks and … had to surrender the contract.

The useless ruff-and-discard

Suppose you need to avoid a loser in this key suit:

♣ AJ97

♣ K1054

An elimination will not necessarily help you. Rather than play on this suit, the defenders may elect to give you a useless ruff-and-discard. You can dispose of one club but will still have to guess where the queen lies.

Such was the club position on the next deal, when Tony partnered Graham Kirby in the 1977 Junior Camrose trophy. England fielded one of the strongest teams on record and beat Ireland, Scotland and Wales by the full 12-0 margin.

North/South Game. Dealer South.

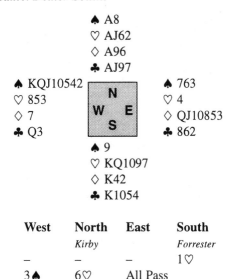

♠ A8
♡ AJ62
◇ A96
♣ AJ97

♠ KQJ10542
♡ 853
◇ 7
♣ Q3

♠ 763
♡ 4
◇ QJ10853
♣ 862

♠ 9
♡ KQ1097
◇ K42
♣ K1054

West	North	East	South
	Kirby		*Forrester*
–	–	–	1♡
3♠	6♡	All Pass	

West led the spade king, won in the dummy. Tony drew trumps in three rounds, West following three times, then ruffed dummy's last spade. When he continued with the ace and king of diamonds, West showed out on the second round. It would not help matters to exit with a third round of diamonds now. East has a complete count on declarer's hand (1-5-3-4) and will surely return another diamond, conceding a ruff-and-discard that will not assist declarer in the slightest.

West's overcall suggested a 7-card suit, in which case his shape would be 7-3-1-2. Tony cashed the ace of clubs and ran the jack of clubs. This lost to the queen but now West had to give a *useful* ruff-and-discard! Away went declarer's diamond loser.

3
GAINING ENTRY

One of many nightmares that inexperienced players face is that of being stuck in the wrong hand. To avoid such a dilemma, forethought may be required as early at trick 1. Tony was declarer in this 3NT contract, from an early round of his team's victorious campaign in the 1987 Gold Cup.

East/West Game. Dealer South.

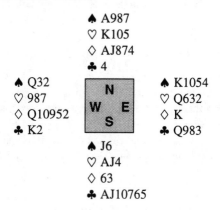

	♠ A987	
	♡ K105	
	◇ AJ874	
	♣ 4	

♠ Q32		♠ K1054
♡ 987		♡ Q632
◇ Q10952		◇ K
♣ K2		♣ Q983

	♠ J6	
	♡ AJ4	
	◇ 63	
	♣ AJ10765	

West	North	East	South
	Brock		*Forrester*
–	–	–	1♣
Pass	1◇	Pass	2♣
Pass	2♠	Pass	2NT
Pass	3NT	All Pass	

West led ♡9 and Tony could count six top tricks when the dummy went down. The club suit was the most likely source of three further tricks, but in that case entries would be needed to the South hand. With this aim in mind, Tony rose with the king of hearts at trick one, preserving his ace-jack.

When ♣4 was led from dummy East followed with the 3. How should declarer tackle the clubs? A finesse of the jack would succeed only when East held both king and queen; it would lose when West held a doubleton honour. Tony decided to rise with the ace of clubs – a play that might also gain when East held a doubleton honour, since the safer East hand would win the second round. He continued with a low club (just as good as the jack, should the suit break 3-3) and was rewarded when the king appeared from West.

A spade switch went to East's king and the spade return drew the jack, queen and ace. Now declarer's care at trick 1 paid off. He crossed to his hand with a heart to the jack and led the jack of clubs, forcing out East's queen. Whether or not East chose to cash ♠10, declarer had nine tricks – four clubs, three hearts, and the two pointed-suit aces.

Entries in the trump suit

One reason for delaying the process of drawing trumps is that you may need to use entries in the trump suit. That was the case here:

North/South Game. Dealer West.

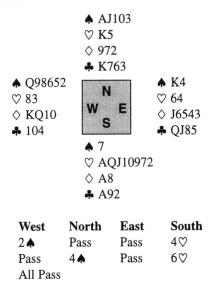

```
              ♠ AJ103
              ♡ K5
              ◇ 972
              ♣ K763
♠ Q98652                  ♠ K4
♡ 83          N           ♡ 64
◇ KQ10      W   E         ◇ J6543
♣ 104         S           ♣ QJ85
              ♠ 7
              ♡ AQJ10972
              ◇ A8
              ♣ A92
```

West	North	East	South
2♠	Pass	Pass	4♡
Pass	4♠	Pass	6♡
All Pass			

North-South brushed aside the Weak Two, South arriving in Six Hearts. West led the king of diamonds, won with the ace. Declarer could see a route home if West held ♠KQ. He would draw trumps and lead a spade towards dummy. If West refused to split, dummy's jack would be finessed and a discard taken on the ace. If instead West split his honours, declarer would win with the ace and return the jack of spades, throwing his losing diamond; the club loser would later be discarded on ♠10.

How likely was it that West had both spade honours, though? He would not have risked a lead from such as ◇Kx if he held the king-queen of spades. And if the diamond lead was indeed from the king-queen, a spade suit headed by the king and queen would give him a hand too strong for a non-vulnerable Weak Two.

Declarer decided to play East for ♠Kx or ♠Qx. At trick 2 he led a spade to the ace. He then ruffed a spade, East's king appearing. Only now did he turn to the trump suit, cashing the ace and king. When both defenders followed, the contract was assured. He led the jack of spades, discarding his diamond loser. He was later able to cross to the club king to discard a club loser on the spade 10.

Dummy's trump suit was unlikely to provide an entry on the next deal, until declarer sprung a trap on the defender in the East seat.

North/South Game. Dealer West.

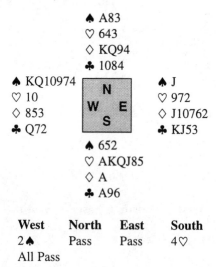

♠ A83
♡ 643
◇ KQ94
♣ 1084

♠ KQ10974
♡ 10
◇ 853
♣ Q72

♠ J
♡ 972
◇ J10762
♣ KJ53

♠ 652
♡ AKQJ85
◇ A
♣ A96

West	North	East	South
2♠	Pass	Pass	4♡
All Pass			

South rushed into Four Hearts when a more circumspect approach might have led to 3NT. Predictably, West's lead of the spade king was awkward, dislodging the only certain entry to the dummy. Unless trumps were 2-2, which would allow declarer to cross to dummy on the third round of the suit, it seemed that dummy's ◊ KQ might wither on the vine. Can you see any way out of the situation?

Hoping to induce an error from East, declarer ducked the first round of spades. The jack appeared from East and West persevered with the queen of spades. Declarer called for dummy's ace and East was quick to pounce with a trump. Big mistake! Declarer won the trump return and drew the outstanding trumps in one more round. He could then unblock the diamond ace and cross to ♡6 to take two discards. East should perhaps have asked himself why declarer was playing in this apparently absurd fashion. Had he looked the other way, refusing to ruff, the contract would have gone down. Even so, credit South for an imaginative shot.

Creating extra entries

A skilled declarer can often conjure an extra entry from thin air. Look at these combinations:

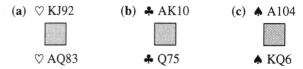

(a) ♡ KJ92   **(b)** ♣ AK10   **(c)** ♠ A104

♡ AQ83   ♣ Q75   ♠ KQ6

In position (a), needing three entries to the North hand, you cash the ace and lead the queen. When West follows, it is safe to overtake with the king; if East shows out, you will finesse the 9 for the third entry. On (b) a degree of risk is involved. If you are desperate for three entries you finesse ♣ 10. You can try the same manoeuvre on (c), leading the 6 for a finesse of the 10. In theory West can thwart you by inserting the jack, but how many defenders are that clever?

Declarer was short of entries to dummy when this grand slam arose:

Love All. Dealer North.

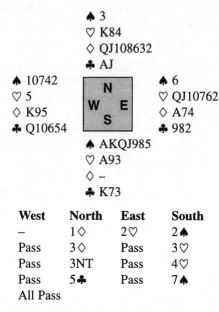

	♠ 3	
	♡ K84	
	◇ QJ108632	
	♣ AJ	
♠ 10742		♠ 6
♡ 5		♡ QJ10762
◇ K95		◇ A74
♣ Q10654		♣ 982
	♠ AKQJ985	
	♡ A93	
	◇ –	
	♣ K73	

West	North	East	South
–	1◇	2♡	2♠
Pass	3◇	Pass	3♡
Pass	3NT	Pass	4♡
Pass	5♣	Pass	7♠
All Pass			

With little justification South barged his way to Seven Spades. West led his singleton heart (a trump would have worked better) and declarer won with the ace. Can you see how to make the contract?

Without East's overcall declarer would doubtless finesse ♣J, discard a heart on the third round of clubs, and attempt to ruff a heart. Such a line is clearly doomed and the only other chance appears to be to set up dummy's diamond suit. Even if diamonds break 3-3 you will need four entries to dummy – three to ruff the suit good, one to reach the established winners. The heart king will provide one entry; you will need three more entries from the club suit.

So, after a suitably deep breath, the play will go: club to the jack, diamond ruff, club to the ace, diamond ruff, *ruff the king of clubs*, take a third diamond ruff. If you survive all that excitement, you will be able to draw trumps and cross to ♡K to discard your heart loser on a good diamond. Ruffing your own winner to create an extra entry is a rare manoeuvre, but hugely satisfying.

Suppose that reaching dummy could be worth two or even three tricks. It may then be worthwhile to sacrifice a trick to pay for the passage:

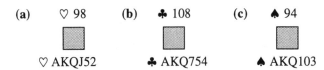

(a)   ♡ 98   (b)   ♣ 108   (c)   ♠ 94

♡ AKQJ52   ♣ AKQ754   ♠ AKQ103

On (a) you can establish a sure entry to dummy by leading low towards the 98. In position (b), again lead a low card from the South hand. If West plays low with a bored expression, try the 8. Combination (c) is slightly different. One of the defenders may well hold four spades to the jack anyway. If you start by leading the 10 from the South hand the defender with Jxxx will have to give ground. If he takes the jack immediately, he sets up the 9 as an entry; if he does not, he waves farewell to his spade trick.

Terence Reese found such a play in the National Pairs many years ago.

Love All. Dealer West.

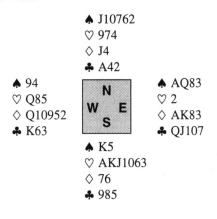

```
                    ♠ J10762
                    ♡ 974
                    ◇ J4
                    ♣ A42
    ♠ 94                         ♠ AQ83
    ♡ Q85          N             ♡ 2
    ◇ Q10952     W   E           ◇ AK83
    ♣ K63          S             ♣ QJ107
                    ♠ K5
                    ♡ AKJ1063
                    ◇ 76
                    ♣ 985
```

West	North	East	South
d'Unienville	*Meredith*	*Truscott*	*Reese*
Pass	Pass	1♠	2♡
Pass	Pass	Dble	All Pass

Nowadays a re-opening double by the opener is a common occurrence, promising little more than a minimum opening even opposite a passed hand. Back in 1951 (yes!) West could expect his partner to hold an above-average opener. Even so, it was a dubious move to pass the double, the more so as +110 from Three Diamonds would outscore +100 for one down doubled against Two Hearts.

West led ♠9, East winning with the ace and returning the suit. Reese won with the king and promptly led ♡10. He had two purposes in mind. Firstly, West might let the card pass. Secondly, if West did capture with the queen, declarer would be able to cross to dummy in the trump suit.

West chose to put up the queen. He then switched to clubs, attacking the ace in dummy. Reese won immediately and ruffed a spade high. He then led a trump and finessed dummy's 7. After ruffing a fourth round of spades high, Reese crossed to the 9 of trumps and discarded a loser on dummy's long spade. A satisfying +470 was the outcome.

How would you have tackled this hand from the 1995 Spring Nationals in New Orleans?

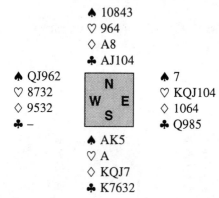

```
                    ♠ 10843
                    ♡ 964
                    ◇ A8
                    ♣ AJ104
    ♠ QJ962           N            ♠ 7
    ♡ 8732                         ♡ KQJ104
    ◇ 9532        W       E        ◇ 1064
    ♣ –               S            ♣ Q985
                    ♠ AK5
                    ♡ A
                    ◇ KQJ7
                    ♣ K7632
```

South reached Six Clubs, East having doubled a 5♡ Blackwood response during the auction. West duly led a heart, declarer winning with the bare ace. If the trumps were no worse than 3-1 the slam would be easy; two spades could be discarded from dummy on the diamonds and a spade ruff would provide the twelfth trick.

In such circumstances there could be no excuse for not considering what would happen if trumps broke 4-0. Nevertheless, several declarers began by cashing the king of trumps. The slam could no longer be made! If a second round of trumps was played to the jack and queen, East would return a third round, preventing declarer from ruffing two hearts in his hand (he would not be able to return to the North hand to draw the last trump). Suppose instead that declarer crossed to the ace of clubs, ruffed a heart, returned to the diamond ace, and ruffed another heart. No good. When he then played a trump to the jack and queen, East would force dummy's last trump with another heart.

Once you spot the problem, the solution is not difficult. At trick 2 you should lead a low trump from the South hand. If West follows, you finesse the jack, knowing that twelve tricks are secure should this lose to the queen. In fact West will show out. Now you rise with the ace and return the jack of trumps. You can draw three rounds of trumps without surrendering the lead. It is then a simple matter to play on diamonds, throwing two spades and then ruffing a spade. East can choose when he takes his trump winner, the only trick for the defence.

The next hand was played by Tony in the 1983 Crockford's Final (which he won with Brock, Armstrong and Kirby). As is often the case, if you could spot the entry problem in time it was not particularly difficult to see the solution too.

East/West Game. Dealer South

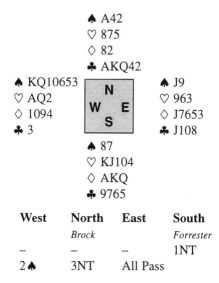

♠ A42
♡ 875
◇ 82
♣ AKQ42

♠ KQ10653
♡ AQ2
◇ 1094
♣ 3

♠ J9
♡ 963
◇ J7653
♣ J108

♠ 87
♡ KJ104
◇ AKQ
♣ 9765

West	North	East	South
	Brock		*Forrester*
–	–	–	1NT
2♠	3NT	All Pass	

West held the first trick with the king of spades, East playing the jack. It was barely possible that West had made a vulnerable Two Spade overcall on a suit of only five cards to the KQ10. Nevertheless, Tony held up the spade ace a second time when West continued spades. Can you see why?

Yes, unless the opposing clubs were 2-2, the suit was blocked. By ducking spades twice, Tony was able to throw the apparently insignificant ♣5 under the spade ace. He could then run five club tricks painlessly, bringing his total to nine.

On some hands you appear to have enough entries but it may still be critical to use them in the right order. Why? Because the defenders may otherwise discard in a key suit, enabling them to overruff you. This is the type of deal we have in mind:

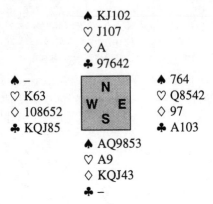

South arrives in Seven Spades, West leading the king of clubs. Had trumps been 2-1, a heart and a diamond could have been ruffed in dummy. But when declarer ruffs the king of clubs and leads a low trump, West shows out. What now?

The solution is a dummy reversal (ruffing four clubs in the South hand, drawing trumps, and scoring four diamond tricks). Let's suppose declarer sets about this with no further thought. He wins the first round of trumps with dummy's 10 and ruffs a second club. He then crosses to the ace of diamonds and ruffs a third club. A trump to dummy's jack brings us to this position:

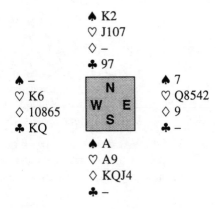

Declarer now takes his final last club ruff. Catastrophe! East will discard ◇9. It will no longer be possible to enter dummy (by ruffing ◇4 with the ♠2) to draw East's last trump.

Declarer needed four entries to the dummy (three to ruff clubs, one to draw East's last trump). Two of these entries, those in the trump suit, were 'safe' – the defenders could not possibly prevent them. The remaining two, the diamond ace and the diamond ruff, were 'unsafe'. They were at risk if East was able to ruff or overruff. The rule in such cases is easy to remember: use the unsafe entries first.

After crossing to the trump 10, revealing the bad trump break, declarer should ruff a club, cross to the diamond ace, and ruff another club. He should then use the remaining unsafe entry, the diamond ruff. When a fourth round of clubs is ruffed with the ace, East can do no damage. The final entry to the dummy, a trump to the king, cannot be put under threat.

4

THE THROW-IN

'On board 21 I made 3NT with a throw-in.' It doesn't sound very glamorous or impressive, does it? That's because of the drab name assigned to the play. Had someone christened it the Assassin's Coup, the play would receive more of the credit it undoubtedly deserves.

Throw-in plays, where you put an opponent on lead and force him to surrender a trick with his return, are often quite difficult to achieve. That's because you usually have to read the opponents' cards accurately. This is not necessarily the case with squeeze or elimination plays.

A throw-in can occur at no-trumps or in a suit contract. If in a suit contract, we assume the element of ruff-and-discard is not present, otherwise it would be termed an elimination play. This is a typical end position, with the lead in the North hand:

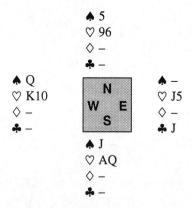

Declarer puts West on lead with a spade and he now has to return a heart into the tenace. You see what we mean by having to read the cards exactly? If West's last three cards were ♠Q, ♡K and ♣J, you would have to play a heart to the ace to make the contract. If his last three cards were ♠Q, ♡10 and ♣J, you would have to take the heart finesse to make the contract. Three possible winning plays in a 3-card ending!

Removing the defender's exit cards

To force the defender to play on the suit where you hold the awaiting tenace, you must first extract his safe exit cards. That was not particularly difficult on this deal, from a 1987 Crockford's match.

East/West Game. Dealer West.

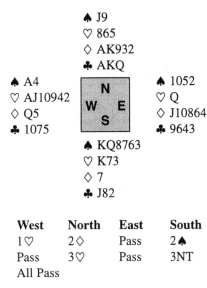

```
               ♠ J9
               ♡ 865
               ◇ AK932
               ♣ AKQ
   ♠ A4                          ♠ 1052
   ♡ AJ10942                     ♡ Q
   ◇ Q5                          ◇ J10864
   ♣ 1075                        ♣ 9643
               ♠ KQ8763
               ♡ K73
               ◇ 7
               ♣ J82
```

West	North	East	South
1♡	2◇	Pass	2♠
Pass	3♡	Pass	3NT
All Pass			

Four Spades looks a better contract but was beaten at the other table when West led ♡A and gave his partner two ruffs. The same lead would have worked well against 3NT, as it happens. This was hard for West to judge; he made the normal lead of the jack of hearts and East produced the queen. East-West were playing a five-card major system, so declarer could rule out the possibility that hearts were 4-4. Hoping that East's ♡Q was a singleton, he held up the king. East switched to a club, won in the dummy, and declarer played the jack of spades. West allowed this card to hold and declarer had to consider his next move carefully. What would you have done?

It would not be productive to play a second spade immediately, since West would have a choice of safe exit cards after taking the ace. Instead declarer cashed dummy's remaining four winners in the minors. Only then did he play a second spade. West won and was left with no escape. He had to play on hearts and declarer ended with an overtrick.

Nine tricks seemed a distant prospect on the next deal, a 3NT from the 1996 Hubert Phillips Bowl final (won for the first time by Tony's team after a mere 26 attempts!).

Love All. Dealer East.

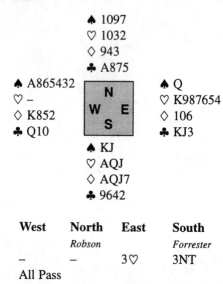

```
                    ♠ 1097
                    ♡ 1032
                    ◊ 943
                    ♣ A875
  ♠ A865432      ┌──────────┐      ♠ Q
  ♡ –            │    N     │      ♡ K987654
  ◊ K852         │ W     E  │      ◊ 106
  ♣ Q10          │    S     │      ♣ KJ3
                 └──────────┘
                    ♠ KJ
                    ♡ AQJ
                    ◊ AQJ7
                    ♣ 9642
```

West	North	East	South
	Robson		*Forrester*
–	–	3♡	3NT
All Pass			

West led ♠2, sneaky but a little too clever since the lead could hardly be from a 4-card suit. Tony took East's queen with the king and saw that he would need extra tricks from all four suits to reach his target. His first move was to play the ace of diamonds followed by the queen. West held off and the hoped-for 10 appeared from East. Tony now played a low club, allowing West's 10 to win. The spade continuation was taken by South's jack and a second round of clubs went to the queen and ace.

The noose was closing around East's neck. Tony finessed the queen of hearts successfully and exited with a club to the king. East had to return a heart, allowing declarer to finesse the jack, and that brought the total to nine tricks: two spades, three hearts, two diamonds and two clubs.

It would not have helped West to win the second round of diamonds and clear the spades. After the pin of East's ◊ 10, dummy's ◊ 9 would be an entry for a second heart finesse. Declarer would score two spades, three hearts, three diamonds and the club ace.

Reading the distribution

To become a competent performer in this arena, you will need to be a good detective – gathering clues from all quarters. Let's see how the Indian maestro, Santanu Ghose, set about the task, playing in the 1996 Macallan International Pairs.

Love All. Dealer North.

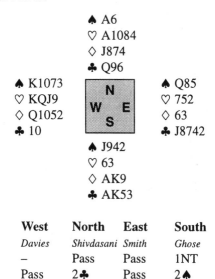

```
              ♠ A6
              ♡ A1084
              ◇ J874
              ♣ Q96
 ♠ K1073                    ♠ Q85
 ♡ KQJ9      N              ♡ 752
 ◇ Q1052   W   E            ◇ 63
 ♣ 10        S              ♣ J8742
              ♠ J942
              ♡ 63
              ◇ AK9
              ♣ AK53
```

West	North	East	South
Davies	*Shivdasani*	*Smith*	*Ghose*
–	Pass	Pass	1NT
Pass	2♣	Pass	2♠
Pass	3NT	All Pass	

Pat Davies led ♡K and Ghose captured with dummy's ace. Ace, king and another diamond came next, Davies winning the third round with the queen and East throwing a heart. Davies cashed a second heart, to avoid being thrown in with a heart later, then exited with a diamond.

Declarer had eight tricks and a 3-3 club break would make it nine. When he cashed ♣A, however, West followed with the 10. West could not afford such a false card from J10x in case East held the king of clubs. Ghose discounted also the chance that the 10 might be an obscure false card from 10xx. Abandoning all hope of the clubs being 3-3, he cashed the king of clubs, West throwing a spade. These cards remained:

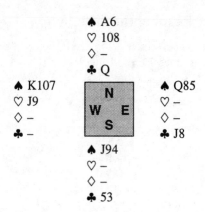

When a club was played to the queen, West could not afford a heart and was forced to discard ♠7. Declarer had a certain count on the minors and could also be fairly sure of the heart position. It followed that West had only two spades at this stage, one of which might well be the king or queen. Ghose's next move was to cash the ace of spades. Pat Davies, West, saw that if she bared the spade king she would be thrown in with it and would have to give a heart trick to dummy. She therefore disposed of the king under dummy's ace. Ghose was not defeated by this. He played a second round of spades towards the jack. East put up the queen and cashed a club but then had to surrender the game-going trick to South's jack of spades.

The throw-in technique is not restricted to no-trumps. Here the contract was an ambitious Six Hearts:

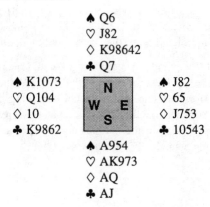

West gave away nothing with his lead, the singleton ◇ 10. Declarer, noting that the contract was not entirely lay-down, won with the ace. When the ace and king of trumps failed to drop the queen, declarer's next idea was to cash the second diamond winner and exit with a trump. If the defender with the trump queen also held both the black kings, he would be end-played.

The plan would have succeeded, had the diamonds divided 3-2. When the diamond queen was led, however, West discarded a club. How would you have proceeded from this point?

Aiming to set up the diamond suit, declarer overtook the diamond queen with dummy's king and called for ◇ 9. East covered with the jack (it is no better to duck) and declarer ruffed in the South hand. West declined to overruff but this did not delay matters for long. He was thrown in with the trump queen on the next trick and had to give an entry to the dummy. Twelve tricks made.

Keep a count on the hand

Sometimes a throw-in will fall into your lap ... provided you have been keeping a count on the hand. Declarer failed the test on this deal:

North/South Game. Dealer East.

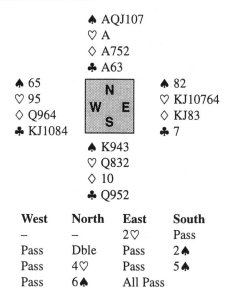

<pre>
              ♠ AQJ107
              ♡ A
              ◇ A752
              ♣ A63
   ♠ 65   ♠ 82
   ♡ 95   N   ♡ KJ10764
   ◇ Q964   W   E   ◇ KJ83
   ♣ KJ1084   S   ♣ 7
              ♠ K943
              ♡ Q832
              ◇ 10
              ♣ Q952
</pre>

West	North	East	South
–	–	2♡	Pass
Pass	Dble	Pass	2♠
Pass	4♡	Pass	5♠
Pass	6♠	All Pass	

East opened with a Weak Two and South eventually arrived in Six Spades, winning the ♡9 lead in the dummy. Viewing prospects from the long-trump hand, North, declarer saw that if he could ruff the three diamond losers he would just require East to hold the king of clubs. Embarking on this plan, he cashed the ace of diamonds, ruffed a diamond low, ruffed a heart, then ruffed a diamond with the 9. A trump to dummy allowed him to ruff the last diamond with the king. After that, he returned to the North hand with a second heart ruff and drew the outstanding trumps.

Rather than banging out the ace of clubs at this stage, declarer paused for thought. East had shown up with two trumps, six hearts, and four diamonds. So ... he held only one club! This was the actual end position:

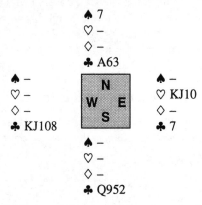

```
              ♠ 7
              ♡ –
              ◇ –
              ♣ A63
   ♠ –                      ♠ –
   ♡ –         N            ♡ KJ10
   ◇ –       W   E          ◇ –
   ♣ KJ108      S           ♣ 7
              ♠ –
              ♡ –
              ◇ –
              ♣ Q952
```

Declarer called for a *low* club from dummy, not caring which singleton came from East (he would cover if the jack or 10 appeared). When East played ♣7, declarer put on the 9 to end-play West.

Declarer started with one particular plan (reverse the dummy, then play ace and another club). As he accumulated evidence on the distribution, he realised that the original strategy could not succeed. This happens quite often. It is pointless to pin your hopes on a lay-out which is no longer possible.

Enemy pre-empts can be a pain in the er ... neck. But if you manage to circumvent them and end in a reasonable contract, you can turn them to your advantage. Reading the cards will normally be easier.

Love All. Dealer East.

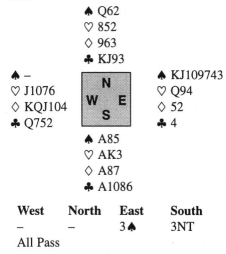

	♠ Q62	
	♡ 852	
	◇ 963	
	♣ KJ93	

♠ –		♠ KJ109743
♡ J1076		♡ Q94
◇ KQJ104		◇ 52
♣ Q752		♣ 4

	♠ A85	
	♡ AK3	
	◇ A87	
	♣ A1086	

West	North	East	South
–	–	3♠	3NT
All Pass			

West attacks in diamonds and you win the third round, East discarding a spade. To have any hope of making the contract, you will need to score four club tricks. Which defender is more likely to hold the queen of clubs?

In the absence of any bidding, you might place East with the card, allowing the 5-2 diamond break to influence you. After East's spade pre-empt, however, East is likely to hold 9 cards in spades and diamonds, West only 5. So, you cash the ace of clubs and run the 10 successfully, East discarding another spade. What now?

You can see four club tricks and four top winners outside. You need a second trick from the spade suit and must therefore arrange an end-play on East. East has no cards left in the minors, so perhaps ace, king and another heart will end-play him. If he wins the third round with ♡Q, he will then have to lead away from the ♠K. But it will not take a genius in the East seat to see this end-play coming. He will surely throw ♡Q under the ace or king, allowing his partner to win the third round of the suit.

To prepare for the throw-in you must make an avoidance play in hearts. Cross to dummy on the third round of clubs and lead a low heart towards the ace. Return to dummy in clubs and lead a low heart towards the king. To escape being end-played with a heart, East will doubtless insert his queen on one of the first two rounds. When he does, let him win the trick. In this way you will be able to play three rounds of hearts without letting West on lead to cash his diamond winners. You reach this end position:

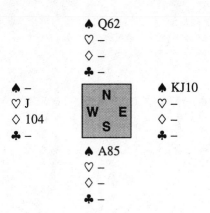

The hard work has been done. You now duck a spade, collecting the last two tricks for the contract.

Plan the card of exit

We will end the chapter with a deal played by former world champion, Nicola Smith, in the 1996 World Mixed Teams championship. Once again accurate play was required to achieve the throw-in.

Love All. Dealer South.

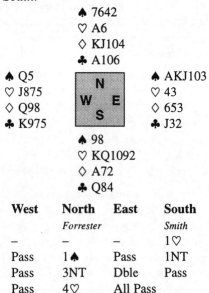

West	North	East	South
	Forrester		*Smith*
–	–	–	1♡
Pass	1♠	Pass	1NT
Pass	3NT	Dble	Pass
Pass	4♡	All Pass	

East doubled 3NT for a spade lead and North wisely decided to try his luck elsewhere. West led the spade queen against Four Hearts and East overtook with the king, continuing with the ace and jack of spades. Since West held two spades to East's five, she was favourite to hold the jack of trumps. Nicola Smith duly ruffed the third round of spades with the king. She next ran the 10 of trumps successfully. A finesse of the other red 10 was equally successful and both defenders followed to the ace of trumps.

Smith re-entered her hand with the ace of diamonds, leaving these cards still out:

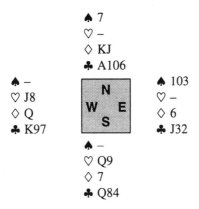

```
                  ♠ 7
                  ♡ –
                  ◇ KJ
                  ♣ A106
   ♠ –              N          ♠ 103
   ♡ J8         W     E        ♡ –
   ◇ Q             S           ◇ 6
   ♣ K97                       ♣ J32
                  ♠ –
                  ♡ Q9
                  ◇ 7
                  ♣ Q84
```

When West produced the 8 on the queen of trumps, declarer (who had already lost two tricks) knew that she had a loser to come in the trump suit. To avoid losing a club trick too, she would need to arrange an end-play on West. Suppose declarer carelessly discards dummy's last spade on the trump queen. That will be one down! After cashing dummy's diamonds, West discarding on the jack, she would have to play clubs herself.

Realising that the spade would be required to perform the actual throw-in, Smith called for a club discard. A diamond to the queen and king was followed by the jack of diamonds. West declined to ruff but declarer could now lead dummy's precious last spade, ruffing in the South hand. It was the end of the road for West. She overruffed with the jack but then had to lead away from the king of clubs.

5

THE CRYSTAL BALL

Against modest opposition you can often make contracts by following an inferior line of play. The defenders could have beaten you, but they weren't quite up to it. Sit down against experts, in a tournament such as the Macallan International Pairs, and the situation is different. The defenders will be very unforgiving any time you stray from the perfect line.

To succeed at the top level, you need to foresee the moves the defenders may make. What do you think of declarer's play on this deal?

Love All. Dealer West.

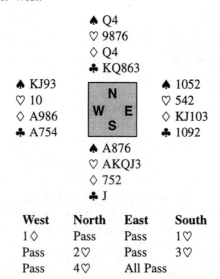

```
                    ♠ Q4
                    ♡ 9876
                    ◇ Q4
                    ♣ KQ863
     ♠ KJ93                      ♠ 1052
     ♡ 10          N             ♡ 542
     ◇ A986      W   E           ◇ KJ103
     ♣ A754        S             ♣ 1092
                    ♠ A876
                    ♡ AKQJ3
                    ◇ 752
                    ♣ J
```

West	North	East	South
1◇	Pass	Pass	1♡
Pass	2♡	Pass	3♡
Pass	4♡	All Pass	

What you might call a limit-bid sequence! Declarer won West's trump lead with the ace and drew a second round, West throwing a diamond. The jack of clubs was taken by West's ace and the defenders now cashed the ace and king of diamonds, followed by a third round of trumps. Declarer was not taxed. He won the trump return in the dummy, discarded two spades on the king and queen of clubs, then ruffed a long club good. A diamond ruff provided access to the established club and away went declarer's last spade. Ten tricks made.

The defence does no better if West underleads the diamond ace after winning the club. Suppose East wins the diamond switch and returns a spade. Declarer puts up the ace, crosses to dummy with a trump and throws his remaining diamonds on the club honours. He can then ruff a club and surrender a spade trick, eventually scoring a spade ruff and the long club.

Well played by declarer, then? Not at all. It was poorly defended. West should have allowed the jack of clubs to win. It would then be too late for declarer to try a spade towards the queen; the defenders would draw a third round of trumps, preventing him from scoring two ruffs in the dummy.

Now we see the best defence, it is not difficult to counter it. The jack of clubs should be led at trick 2. If West ducks then, you can play a spade towards the queen, later taking two ruffs in the dummy. (The defenders have to cash their diamond tricks immediately, or you will throw one on the spade ace.)

The next deal would have caused no problem at the local church hall. Tony was facing stiffer opposition in the 1995 Iceland Open.

East/West Game. Dealer North.

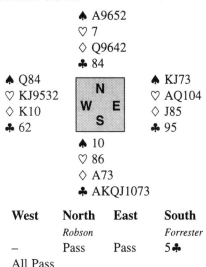

West	North	East	South
	Robson		*Forrester*
–	Pass	Pass	5♣
All Pass			

West led ♣2 and East played the 5 rather than the 9, careful not to set up an extra entry to dummy. No more trumps could be drawn at this stage, since dummy's remaining trump controlled the heart suit.

At trick 2 Tony led a low diamond. No problem at St Bartholomew's – West would go in with the king and cash at most one heart, after which declarer could draw trumps and run the diamonds.

Defenders in the frozen North are not so obliging. After some agony West contributed ◊ 10. It may seem 'automatic' to win with dummy's queen, but Tony saw that there would then be no way to arrive at eleven tricks. The only hope was that the king of diamonds was doubleton. Tony called for a low diamond from dummy, allowing West's ◊ 10 to win. The defenders were powerless. When declarer regained the lead he would draw trumps, drop West's diamond king with the ace, and cash the diamond suit.

We move now to the 1977 Bermuda Bowl. Suppose you had held Fred Hamilton's cards in the South seat. Would you have spotted any impending danger?

Game All. Dealer West.

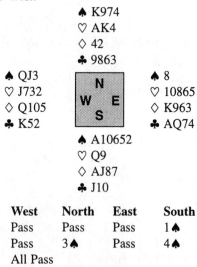

<pre>
                    ♠ K974
                    ♡ AK4
                    ◊ 42
                    ♣ 9863
    ♠ QJ3   ♠ 8
    ♡ J732   N   ♡ 10865
    ◊ Q105   W   E   ◊ K963
    ♣ K52   S   ♣ AQ74
                    ♠ A10652
                    ♡ Q9
                    ◊ AJ87
                    ♣ J10
</pre>

West	North	East	South
Pass	Pass	Pass	1♠
Pass	3♠	Pass	4♠
All Pass			

With no opposition bidding, Hamilton opened One Spade in the fourth seat and reached Four Spades. Had West found a club lead, you would not now be reading about the hand. West's opening shot was a less inspired ♡2 and declarer won with the queen. How would you have tackled the hand?

Without touching the trump suit, Hamilton played two more rounds of hearts, discarding one of his club losers. He then led a diamond from dummy, the jack losing to the queen. When the defenders played on clubs, declarer ruffed the second round and cashed the ace and king of trumps. He could now proceed with his cross-ruff, ruffing two clubs in the South hand, two diamonds in dummy. At some time during this process West could score his master trump, the last trick for the defence.

That may have looked fairly easy but suppose declarer had pulled just one round of trumps before beginning his preparations. West would then have been able to play a second and third round of trumps when he gained the lead in clubs and diamonds.

Success on the next deal, from the 1992 Olympiad in Salsamaggiore, depended on reading the defenders' minds.

Love All. Dealer North.

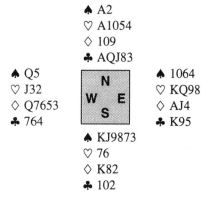

```
                    ♠ A2
                    ♡ A1054
                    ◊ 109
                    ♣ AQJ83
      ♠ Q5                      ♠ 1064
      ♡ J32          N          ♡ KQ98
      ◊ Q7653    W     E        ◊ AJ4
      ♣ 764          S          ♣ K95
                    ♠ KJ9873
                    ♡ 76
                    ◊ K82
                    ♣ 102
```

West	North	East	South
	Robson		*Forrester*
–	1♣	Pass	1♠
Pass	2♣	Pass	2♠
Pass	3♠	Pass	4♠
All Pass			

East won the ◊ 5 lead with the ace and switched to the king of hearts. Tony captured with dummy's ace and crossed to the king of diamonds to run ♣ 10. This lost to the king and East cashed the queen of hearts – the third trick for the defence. He continued with a third heart, ruffed in the South hand, and all now depended on picking up the trump suit. Any ideas?

Tony crossed to the ace of trumps and played a second trump to the king, dropping West's queen. After drawing East's last trump with the jack, he could claim ten tricks. Why play in this way, apparently against the odds? There were two indications. The first was that East had already shown up with 13 or 14 points outside the trump suit (♡KQ, ◇A, ♣K, and he was marked with ◇J or ◇Q after West's lead of a low diamond). If East held the spade queen as well he might have doubled the opening bid or overcalled 1NT. A more powerful clue lay in East's chosen line of defence. Had he started with ♠Qxx, he would surely have played a third round of diamonds, forcing the dummy to ruff.

Many a disaster can be thwarted ... if you see it coming in time! Tony played this hand in the Gold Cup back in 1982.

Game All. Dealer North.

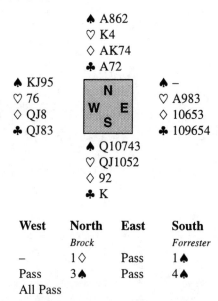

	♠ A862	
	♡ K4	
	◇ AK74	
	♣ A72	
♠ KJ95		♠ −
♡ 76		♡ A983
◇ QJ8		◇ 10653
♣ QJ83		♣ 109654
	♠ Q10743	
	♡ QJ1052	
	◇ 92	
	♣ K	

West	North	East	South
	Brock		*Forrester*
−	1◇	Pass	1♠
Pass	3♠	Pass	4♠
All Pass			

West led the queen of clubs, Tony winning with the king. The contract looks safe enough but once in a while West will hold all four trumps. Since this was the only real risk to the contract, declarer would have no excuse if he failed to counter it. At trick 2 Tony led ♠3. When West followed with the 5, the 6 was played from dummy. When East showed out declarer could claim the contract, conceding one heart and two trump tricks.

There was some chance that hearts would be 5-1 and that East might win the trump finesse, return his singleton heart and receive a heart ruff. This would not have put the contract in danger, however; declarer would lose at most the heart ace and two trump tricks. Finessing dummy's ♠6 was a perfect safety play.

When the opponents hold seven cards in a suit, what is the chance that they will break 6-1? The mathematical tables tell us it is 6.8%, low enough to be ignored in the mind of a certain type of player. But in some circumstances this risk can swell alarmingly. Look at this deal:

East/West Game. Dealer South.

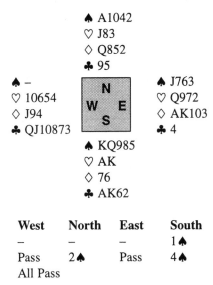

```
              ♠ A1042
              ♡ J83
              ◇ Q852
              ♣ 95
   ♠ -                    ♠ J763
   ♡ 10654       N        ♡ Q972
   ◇ J94      W     E     ◇ AK103
   ♣ QJ10873      S       ♣ 4
              ♠ KQ985
              ♡ AK
              ◇ 76
              ♣ AK62
```

West	North	East	South
–	–	–	1♠
Pass	2♠	Pass	4♠
All Pass			

West leads the queen of clubs against Four Spades and you win with the ace. When you play the king of trumps West discards a club. How would you continue from this point?

The original declarer played the king of clubs next, cursing his luck when East ruffed. There was no way to recover; he had two certain diamond losers and could not avoid a further loser in clubs.

The risk of a 6-1 club break on this deal was far greater than the bare percentage we quoted. When the opening lead is an honour, this will normally be from a sequence. A reasonable way to assess the likely club break on such hands is to allocate the QJ10 to West, then share the remaining cards between the two defenders. So, the chance of a 6-1 break is more like the normal chance of a 3-1 break (West holding three, East one). That's about 1-in-4! On the present deal this was confirmed by East holding four trumps to his partner's nil and by West's willingness to discard a small club on the first round of trumps.

Had declarer realised how great the danger was, he might have made more effort to cope with it. On some hands the answer would be to lead the second round of clubs from the dummy; it would not help East to ruff a loser and with the club king safely in the bag you could ruff one of your club losers with the ace. Here, though, you cannot afford to use the ace of trumps as an entry to lead towards your clubs. East would then be able to overruff twice in the club suit. The only way to make the contract is to duck the second round of clubs! When you regain the lead you ruff the remaining low club with the ace and pick up East's trump holding by leading dummy's 10.

Andy Robson had to reach for the crystal ball as early as trick 1 on this deal from the 1996 Reisinger Teams in San Francisco:

Love All. Dealer South.

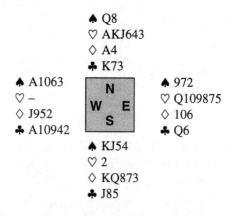

| ♠ Q8 |
| ♡ AKJ643 |
| ◇ A4 |
| ♣ K73 |

♠ A1063		♠ 972
♡ –		♡ Q109875
◇ J952		◇ 106
♣ A10942		♣ Q6

| ♠ KJ54 |
| ♡ 2 |
| ◇ KQ873 |
| ♣ J85 |

West	North	East	South
	Forrester		*Robson*
–	–	–	Pass
Pass	1♡	Pass	1♠
Dble	3♡	Pass	3NT
All Pass			

When ♣4 appeared on the table it was already possible to form a picture of West's hand. He was likely to hold the spade ace and a five-card club suit. With a holding as strong as ♣AQxxx he might have opened the bidding. It was possible that he had ♣Q10xxx, but in that case East would beat the contract by winning the first round with the ace and clearing the suit. No, the best chance was surely that West held ♣A10xxx and the club suit could be blocked.

At trick 1 Robson made the fine play of rising with dummy's king of clubs, East playing the 6. The queen of spades was allowed to hold. West won the second round of spades and played a club to East's queen. Robson won the switch back to spades and tested the diamond suit, finding West with four. In the 4-card ending he led a heart towards dummy. When West showed out he inserted dummy's 6, end-playing East to return a heart.

There was no problem with reading the cards on the next deal, since West had opened with a strong no-trump. Declarer still had to predict what moves the defence would make and how he could counter them.

Love All. Dealer West.

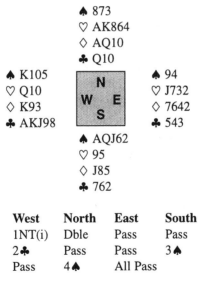

	♠ 873	
	♡ AK864	
	◇ AQ10	
	♣ Q10	
♠ K105		♠ 94
♡ Q10		♡ J732
◇ K93		◇ 7642
♣ AKJ98		♣ 543
	♠ AQJ62	
	♡ 95	
	◇ J85	
	♣ 762	

West	North	East	South
1NT(i)	Dble	Pass	Pass
2♣	Pass	Pass	3♠
Pass	4♠	All Pass	

   (i)   15-17 points

West starts with the ace, king and jack of clubs. Declarer ruffs with dummy's 8 and is relieved to see East follow suit. What now?

If declarer plays a trump to the queen the finesse will lose (as indicated by West's opening bid). West will then play a fourth round of clubs allowing East to uppercut with the 9 of trumps. West's 10 of trumps will be promoted into the setting trick. Suppose instead he plays the ace and queen of trumps. This will prevent any trump promotion but another danger lurks. West will exit with a heart to the dummy and the only route back to your hand will be to ruff a third round of hearts. One down! West has only two hearts and will overruff.

Our glimpse into the crystal ball has revealed the dangers of the hand. How can they be avoided? Declarer must cash the ace and king of hearts first and only then play the ace and queen of trumps. Now West cannot lock declarer in the dummy. Declarer can win West's return, draw the last trump and claim the remainder.

5
THE TRUMP COUP

Suppose you reach an over-ambitious Seven Spades. The side suits are solid but the trump suit lies like this:

You cash the king and finesse the jack successfully, but West shows out. Since no trump remains in dummy to repeat the finesse, the only chance of avoiding a loser is to reach an ending such as this:

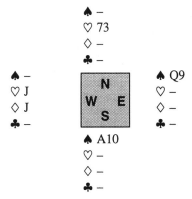

You lead a heart from dummy and score the last two tricks.

How can such an end position be reached? The first point to note is that at the crucial moment you must have the same number of trumps as the defender involved. If you held three trumps to East's two in the position above, you would have to ruff at trick 11 and lead away from your trump tenace. Secondly, you have to manage the entries so that you are in dummy at the key moment, in order to lead a plain card towards your trump tenace.

Let's see how it works at the table.

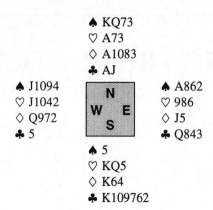

♠ KQ73
♡ A73
◇ A1083
♣ AJ

♠ J1094
♡ J1042
◇ Q972
♣ 5

♠ A862
♡ 986
◇ J5
♣ Q843

♠ 5
♡ KQ5
◇ K64
♣ K109762

South opens on an 11-count and North refuses to drop the bidding until 6♣ is reached. West leads ♠J, covered by the king and ace, and East switches to ♡9. South can finesse either defender for the trump queen. A technician will play East for the queen, however, because there will then be some chance of making the contract even when trumps break 4-1.

Realising that entries will be needed to dummy, declarer begins by winning the heart switch with the king. He then crosses to the ace of trumps and runs the trump jack. Good news and bad news. The finesse succeeds but West shows out. Declarer must now aim for a trump coup. To reduce his trump length to the same as East's (a prime requirement, remember), he must ruff two spades. Declarer plays the queen of spades, discarding a diamond, then ruffs a spade. All follow to the queen and ace of hearts and declarer ruffs another spade. He cashes the king and ace of diamonds, East following obediently, and surveys the following satisfying end position:

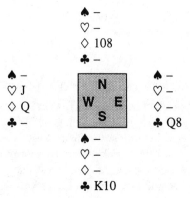

♠ —
♡ —
◇ 108
♣ —

♠ —
♡ J
◇ Q
♣ —

♠ —
♡ —
◇ —
♣ Q8

♠ —
♡ —
◇ —
♣ K10

A diamond lead from dummy guillotines the trump queen.

A similar effect is sometimes achieved by an end-play. You exit at trick 11 and score the last two tricks with your well-placed tenace in trumps. Suppose we alter the previous deal slightly:

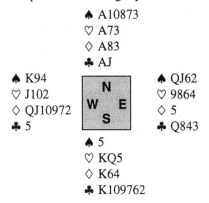

♠ A10873
♡ A73
◇ A83
♣ AJ

♠ K94
♡ J102
◇ QJ10972
♣ 5

♠ QJ62
♡ 9864
◇ 5
♣ Q843

♠ 5
♡ KQ5
◇ K64
♣ K109762

Once again South is in Six Clubs, this time after West has made a weak jump overcall in diamonds. West leads the diamond queen and declarer wins with dummy's ace (a key move, as we will see later). Declarer should bear in mind that East may well hold four trumps to the queen. Since entries to dummy are not plentiful, he should start to reduce his trumps immediately. At trick 2 he cashes the ace of spades and ruffs a spade – fairly safe, since West might have led a singleton spade. Now comes a trump to the ace and the jack of trumps. As before, the jack is run successfully but West shows out. Declarer ruffs another spade, reducing his trumps to the same length as East's, then cashes three rounds of hearts, ending in the dummy. This is the position:

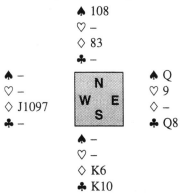

♠ 108
♡ –
◇ 83
♣ –

♠ –
♡ –
◇ J1097
♣ –

♠ Q
♡ 9
◇ –
♣ Q8

♠ –
♡ –
◇ K6
♣ K10

A spade towards the trump tenace would not be good enough; declarer would score his two trumps but lose the last two tricks. Instead he leads a diamond towards the king. (That was why the diamond lead had to be taken in the dummy.) It would not help East to ruff a loser, so he discards. Declarer wins with the king and exits with his diamond loser. His ♣K10, poised over East's ♣Q8, are certain to score the last two tricks. Note that once again it was necessary to reduce South's trumps to the same length as the key defender's.

Promoting the long trump holding

When the adverse trump holding lies under the long trumps, some surprising results can be achieved. East must have felt confident of defeating Six Spades on this deal:

North/South Game. Dealer South.

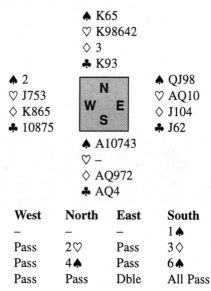

```
                    ♠ K65
                    ♡ K98642
                    ◇ 3
                    ♣ K93
     ♠ 2                           ♠ QJ98
     ♡ J753          N             ♡ AQ10
     ◇ K865       W     E          ◇ J104
     ♣ 10875         S             ♣ J62
                    ♠ A10743
                    ♡ –
                    ◇ AQ972
                    ♣ AQ4
```

West	North	East	South
–	–	–	1♠
Pass	2♡	Pass	3◇
Pass	4♠	Pass	6♠
Pass	Pass	Dble	All Pass

Reading the double as Lightner, West led a low heart. Declarer ruffed East's queen and paused to plan the play. If spades were 3-2, and the diamonds 4-3 with the king onside, the contract could be made by straightforward play. He would finesse the diamond queen, ruff the suit good with two ruffs, cash the two top trumps, and concede just one trump.

However, East's heart honours alone would not justify a double and declarer suspected that the trumps would break unfavourably. He decided to play for four top winners in the minors, plus eight trump tricks. He began by playing three rounds of clubs (otherwise the defenders might be able to discard a club while he cross-ruffed in the red suits). He then cashed the ace of diamonds and ruffed a diamond. Heart ruff, diamond ruff, heart ruff, brought him to this position, with the lead in the South hand:

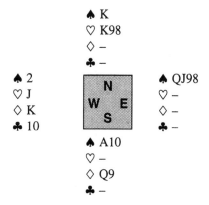

Declarer ruffed a diamond with the king, East underruffing, and played a heart. Had South's remaining trumps been ♠ AJ, this would have been a straightforward trump coup against East's queen. As the cards lay, South's ♠ A10 proved equally effective. East had to split his honours, to prevent declarer ruffing with the 10. Rather than overruffing, South discarded his remaining diamond; he could then finesse on East's enforced trump return. In effect, declarer promoted the trump holding in the South hand, by leading a plain card towards it.

Despite setting out with a different idea in mind, Tony achieved a similar ending on this deal from a 1983 Gold Cup semi-final against Rob Sheehan's team:

Game All. Dealer East.

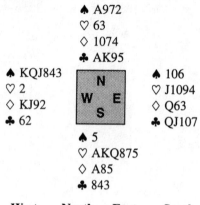

♠ A972
♡ 63
◇ 1074
♣ AK95

♠ KQJ843
♡ 2
◇ KJ92
♣ 62

♠ 106
♡ J1094
◇ Q63
♣ QJ107

♠ 5
♡ AKQ875
◇ A85
♣ 843

West	North	East	South
	Brock		*Forrester*
–	–	Pass	1♡
1♠	2♣	Pass	2♡
Pass	2NT	Pass	4♡
All Pass			

Tony won the spade king lead in dummy and immediately ruffed a spade. His general idea was to score the 8, 7 and 5 of trumps by ruffing spades, thereby overcoming a possible bad break in the trump suit. The ace and king of trumps were cashed, revealing that East had indeed started with four trumps. Tony crossed to the ace of clubs and led another spade. If East were to ruff (from his remaining J10 in trumps), declarer would simply discard a diamond and be able to draw trumps when he regained the lead. East therefore discarded and Tony ruffed with the 7. He returned to dummy with the club king and led the last spade towards his ♡Q8. East could not defend the position. If he ruffed, declarer would discard; if he discarded, declarer would score ♡8, bringing his total to six trumps and four side-suit winners.

At the other table the declarer (it would be unfair to name him) failed to ruff a spade at trick 2. When the bad trump break came to light, Zia – oh dear, the name slipped out – had insufficient entries to dummy to achieve the trump coup.

How many winners should you cash?

There is one further problem we need to address. When you are about to run an established side suit in the dummy, how many winners should you cash in the other suits first? Look at this deal, for example:

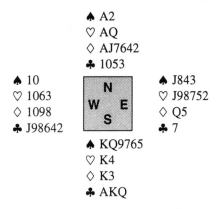

You bid splendidly to Seven Spades and West leads ◇ 10, won in the South hand. A trump to the ace draws the 10 from West. It would not be good play to finesse the 9 on the second round of trumps ('Restricted Choice made single 10 more likely than J10 doubleton, partner'), since you would then pay out to J10x with West too.

We'll assume that you return to the king of trumps, not pleased to see West show out. Your only chance now is to shorten your trumps to match East's, by ruffing two diamonds. You will then return to dummy to lead the remaining diamonds through East's ♠J8. The question is: how many rounds of clubs should you cash first?

After ruffing two diamonds you will have two winning diamonds left, good for two club discards (should East decide not to ruff in). So, you need to cash only *one* club before playing on diamonds. On the layout shown you would go down immediately if you attempted to cash more than one club, since East would ruff. If instead you failed to cash any clubs, East would discard his singleton club when you took the first diamond ruff. You would then reach this dead-end position:

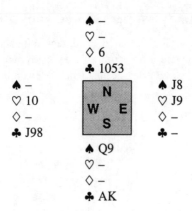

East would discard on the last diamond. You would have to play a club and East would strike with a trump.

Backward trump coup

Suppose you are in Six Spades, with no outside losers and this trump suit:

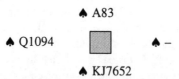

♠ A93

♠ Q1084

♠ –

♠ KJ7652

No problem, if you know your safety plays! You cash the king first, then lead low, finessing dummy's 9 if West plays low. Should West show out on the first round, you would rise with the ace on the second round, then lead towards the jack.

Let's make things a little more difficult, strengthening West's holding:

♠ A83

♠ Q1094

♠ –

♠ KJ7652

Now you cannot avoid two losers by straightforward play. You would have to plan an end-play on West.

West suffered such a fate on this deal:

Love All. Dealer North.

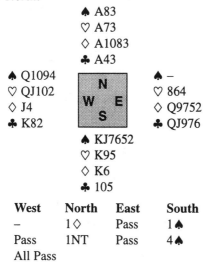

♠ A83
♡ A73
◊ A1083
♣ A43

♠ Q1094   ♠ –
♡ QJ102   ♡ 864
◊ J4   ◊ Q9752
♣ K82   ♣ QJ976

♠ KJ7652
♡ K95
◊ K6
♣ 105

West	North	East	South
–	1◊	Pass	1♠
Pass	1NT	Pass	4♠
All Pass			

West led ♡Q and the contract looked comfortable until East showed out on the ace of trumps. Declarer turned his mind towards an end-play on West. At trick 3 he ducked a club, East winning with the queen. The heart return was taken with the king and declarer crossed to the ace of clubs and ruffed a club. When this passed by without mishap, he cashed the king and ace of diamonds successfully. These cards remained:

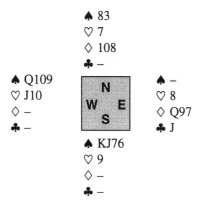

♠ 83
♡ 7
◊ 108
♣ –

♠ Q109   ♠ –
♡ J10   ♡ 8
◊ –   ◊ Q97
♣ –   ♣ J

♠ KJ76
♡ 9
◊ –
♣ –

West was thrown in with a heart and could do no better than return his last heart. Declarer ruffed with the 6 and exited with the 7 of trumps, end-playing West for the second time.

A bad trump break was announced during the bidding on this deal from the 1996 Macallan International Pairs.

Game All. Dealer West.

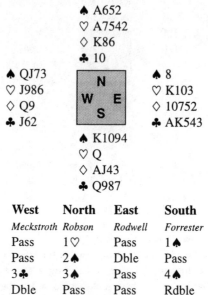

West	North	East	South
Meckstroth	*Robson*	*Rodwell*	*Forrester*
Pass	1♡	Pass	1♠
Pass	2♠	Dble	Pass
3♣	3♠	Pass	4♠
Dble	Pass	Pass	Rdble
All Pass			

Tony won the ◇Q lead with the ace and conceded a club to West's jack. He won the diamond continuation with the jack, ruffed a club, and cashed the ace of hearts. Heart ruff, club ruff, heart ruff, produced this ending, with South on lead:

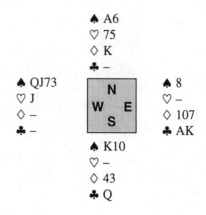

When Tony led ♣Q he could not be prevented from scoring three more trump tricks. If West threw a heart, he would score ♠6 immediately. If West ruffed with an honour, he would discard ◇K and eventually score ♠10 on any return. Meckstroth ruffed with ♠7, but now Tony could overruff with the ace and ruff a heart. Ten tricks!

7

THE SQUEEZE

No play has a greater aura than the squeeze, many believing it to be the pinnacle of expert card-play. In truth most squeezes are not at all difficult to perform. You need to be familiar with a few basics, it's true, and we will cover that ground first.

This is a typical position, with North on lead:

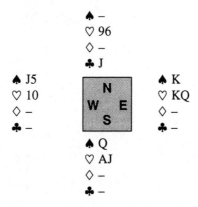

On dummy's last club, East has no card to spare. He is squeezed, forced to surrender one of his guards. What was the cause of his embarrassment? He had to find a discard *before* South. Give the two guards to West instead and the squeeze would not work. South would have to throw one of his threat cards and West would then have a safe discard. Such an ending is therefore known as a positional squeeze.

Squeeze endings nearly always have these three components:

    (a)   A squeeze card – the card that forces the fatal discard
    (b)   A single threat
    (c)   An extended threat – a threat card accompanied by a winner

In the position above, ♣J was the squeeze card, ♠Q was the single threat, South's ♡AJ was the extended threat. When the single threat lies opposite the extended threat, it may be possible to squeeze either opponent:

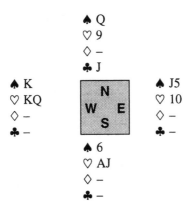

The squeeze card (♣J) is led and this time the guards lie with West rather than East. No problem! The South hand can spare ♠6 and West is squeezed. What caused West's embarrassment in this case? It was not the position of his cards, it was the fact that he could not hold in one hand as many cards as declarer could in two. Such an ending is known as an 'automatic squeeze'.

There are a few more basics to cover but, before you nod off, we will look at a real-life squeeze hand. It was one that required some detective work early in the play.

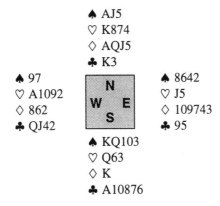

South arrived in 6NT and West led ♦6 (second best from a bad suit), won in the South hand. Declarer could count ten top tricks outside the heart suit. One possible saviour was to find a defender with ace doubleton of hearts; if declarer could guess which defender had this holding he could lead a small card through the ace and duck on the next round, scoring two heart tricks. Hoping to gain some clue to the heart distribution, declarer crossed to the spade ace and cashed two more rounds of diamonds. Both defenders followed and declarer threw two clubs from the South hand. When the three remaining spades were cashed, West showed out on the third round, throwing a club, then a heart. A question for you – from West's discards, how would you expect the diamonds to be divided?

Surely West started with only three diamonds. Otherwise he would have discarded his diamonds, rather than deplete his holdings in your key suits. So, West started with two spades (known) and three diamonds (we reckon). He has thrown one card from each of the other suits and we can therefore almost 'see' that he started with 2-4-3-4 shape. Although East may have started with ace doubleton of hearts in this case, there is no need to lead towards the queen in the South hand. With a heart-club squeeze on West in your mind, you lead the queen of hearts from the South hand. West captures and returns a heart. You win with dummy's king and survey this position:

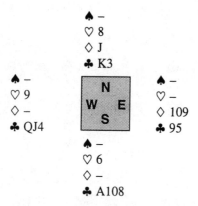

You lead ◇J (the squeeze card), throwing ♡6 from your hand. West has no good card to play.

Interesting, isn't it, how it was possible to reconstruct West's most likely shape? This was partly by observation (when West showed out of a suit), partly by deduction (when he discarded in a particular way), and partly by necessity (the slam could not be made if hearts were 3-3, so we assumed they were 4-2).

Rectifying the count

Time for another 'basic technique'. Let's look at the play in 6NT on this deal:

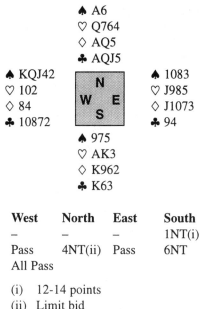

```
              ♠ A6
              ♡ Q764
              ◇ AQ5
              ♣ AQJ5
♠ KQJ42                      ♠ 1083
♡ 102          N             ♡ J985
◇ 84        W     E          ◇ J1073
♣ 10872        S             ♣ 94
              ♠ 975
              ♡ AK3
              ◇ K962
              ♣ K63
```

West	North	East	South
–	–	–	1NT(i)
Pass	4NT(ii)	Pass	6NT
All Pass			

(i)   12-14 points
(ii) Limit bid

Slightly ambitious calling by both participants but the hands fitted well and 6NT was a good contract. West led the king of spades, won in the dummy, and declarer tested the heart suit. No luck there, East had started with four. All now seemed to depend on the diamond suit; it might be divided 3-3, or a doubleton jack or 10 might fall from West, giving declarer the option of a finesse. Declarer cashed the ace and queen of diamonds but no honour came from West. Another thought now occurred to him. Perhaps East had started with four diamonds along with his four hearts and could be squeezed. Yes, it must be right to take the clubs now, to put East under pressure. This was the position as declarer played dummy's last club:

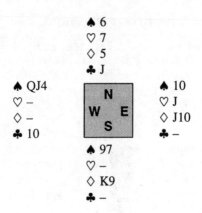

Declarer had a squeeze-card (♣J), a single threat (♡7), and an extended threat (♢K9). The two red-suit guards were held by the same defender, too. In declarer's eyes it looked good for a squeeze but when he led the club jack something went wrong. East was not under any pressure, he simply threw ♠10. Declarer had to concede the last two tricks and that was one down. Some would unkindly say that the play had matched the bidding!

Why did the squeeze fail to operate? Because East had a spare card in his hand – the position was not 'tight'. If East's extra card had been removed earlier in the play, all would have been well. Suppose that declarer makes the apparently strange move of ducking West's king of spades at trick 1. This will draw a spade from East's hand. When declarer wins the continuation and follows the same path as before, the end position will be crucially different:

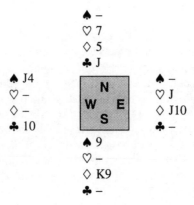

Everyone has one spade fewer. The end position is now tight and East will indeed be squeezed when the club jack if played from dummy.

So, when you are aiming for a squeeze it is generally beneficial to lose at an early stage those tricks which you can afford to lose. If you are aiming for twelve tricks, you will need to lose one trick early on. If your target is nine, you will need to lose four. As we have seen, the purpose is to tighten the end position, so the defenders will have no spare cards.

This process of deliberately losing tricks early in the play is known as 'rectifying the count'. David Johnston, of Northern Ireland, used the technique to good effect in a 1996 Camrose match against England.

Love All. Dealer West.

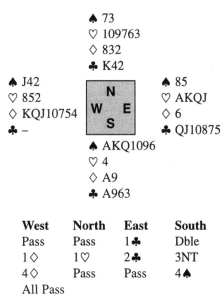

```
                    ♠ 73
                    ♡ 109763
                    ◇ 832
                    ♣ K42
   ♠ J42                         ♠ 85
   ♡ 852            N            ♡ AKQJ
   ◇ KQJ10754    W     E         ◇ 6
   ♣ –              S            ♣ QJ10875
                    ♠ AKQ1096
                    ♡ 4
                    ◇ A9
                    ♣ A963
```

West	North	East	South
Pass	Pass	1♣	Dble
1◇	1♡	2♣	3NT
4◇	Pass	Pass	4♠
All Pass			

The English West was reticent on the first two rounds but then managed to dislodge South from the safe 3NT into a much trickier Four Spades.

Johnston won the diamond lead, drew trumps in three rounds, and led a heart. East won the trick and saw that a heart-club squeeze was looming. In an effort to break up the entries, he switched to the queen of clubs. When Johnston allowed this card to win, East could not play another club without allowing South's 9 to score. He therefore switched back to hearts, leading the ace. Johnston allowed this card to win too, discarding a diamond. There were two purposes behind this second duck. It would rectify the count for a squeeze; it would also force East to play yet another heart, killing West's guard if he held such as ♡Qxx opposite East's ♡AKJx.

Declarer ruffed the third round of hearts and ran his remaining trumps. This was the ending:

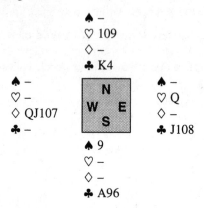

```
                  ♠ –
                  ♡ 109
                  ◇ –
                  ♣ K4
   ♠ –                         ♠ –
   ♡ –           N             ♡ Q
   ◇ QJ107     W     E         ◇ –
   ♣ –           S             ♣ J108
                  ♠ 9
                  ♡ –
                  ◇ –
                  ♣ A96
```

A heart was thrown from dummy on the last trump and East had no good discard.

Does the topic of squeeze play still seem rather forboding? See what you make of a couple of basic squeeze hands. In both cases try to spot the squeeze-card, the single threat, and the extended threat. Ask yourself also which defender(s) may become squeezed.

Problem I

```
West                              East
♠ J76              N              ♠ A52
♡ A6          W         E         ♡ KQ82
◇ AKQJ92          S              ◇ 10753
♣ A3                              ♣ K9
```

Contract: 7◇ by West. Lead: ♠K.

Answer: You win the spade lead, draw trumps, and run the remaining winners in the minors. The opening lead marks North with ♠Q. If he also holds four hearts he will be squeezed by the last minor-suit card. The squeeze card is ♣A, the single threat is ♠J, the extended threat is dummy's heart holding.

Problem II

West		East
♠ K82		♠ A753
♡ AQJ3		♡ K104
◇ 952		◇ AK4
♣ A103		♣ KQ5

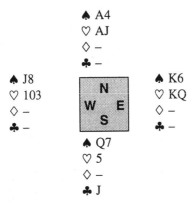

Contract: 6NT by West. Lead: ◇ Q.

Answer: You win the diamond lead and duck a round of spades. The purpose is two-fold: if the suit breaks 3-3 it will yield a twelfth trick directly; also, the count had been rectified for a possible squeeze. Let's say that North wins the spade trick and returns ◇ J. You win with the king and cash four rounds of hearts, throwing ◇ 4, followed by three rounds of clubs. If either defender (presumably North) holds ◇ 10 and four spades, he will be squeezed. The squeeze card is ♣A, the single threat is ◇ 9, the extended threat is dummy's spade suit.

The Vienna Coup

Something interesting happened during the play of that last hand. North's two plays in diamonds removed the ace and king of diamonds from the dummy (East). That worked to declarer's benefit. West's ◇ 9 was freed to act as a threat against either defender.

Sometimes declarer needs to cash one or more high cards in this way himself. Look at this end position:

```
              ♠ A4
              ♡ AJ
              ◇ -
              ♣ -
  ♠ J8                    ♠ K6
  ♡ 103        N          ♡ KQ
  ◇ -       W     E       ◇ -
  ♣ -          S          ♣ -
              ♠ Q7
              ♡ 5
              ◇ -
              ♣ J
```

East guards both the majors and it seems that we may be able to embarrass him. We lead the squeeze card, the ♣ J, and a small problem emerges –

what can we throw from dummy? There is no good answer. If we discard
♠4, East can safely bare the spade king. We cannot then untangle two
spade tricks and the squeeze will fail.

Suppose, in a moment of inspiration, we had cashed the ace of spades
earlier in the play. The layout would have been very much to our liking:

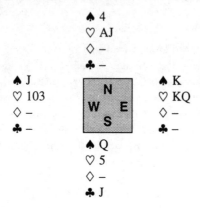

```
                    ♠ 4
                    ♡ AJ
                    ◊ –
                    ♣ –
  ♠ J                             ♠ K
  ♡ 103                           ♡ KQ
  ◊ –                             ◊ –
  ♣ –                             ♣ –
                    ♠ Q
                    ♡ 5
                    ◊ –
                    ♣ J
```

You see how removing the spade ace has freed our ♠Q to act as a threat
against East? Now we can throw dummy's ♠4 and East will have to wave
the white flag. The ace of spades was in our way – blocking the suit. By
cashing it in good time, we freed the way for the squeeze. This piece of
magic is known as the Vienna Coup.

Isolating the guard

Sometimes both defenders start with a guard in one of your side suits. By
ruffing a round or two, you may be able to remove one defender's cover.
Suppose you have a side suit distributed like this:

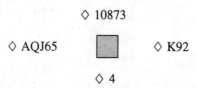

```
                    ◊ 10873
  ◊ AQJ65                         ◊ K92
                    ◊ 4
```

Both defenders guard the diamonds and a squeeze may not be possible.
However, suppose you give up a diamond and ruff two diamonds. The
situation will then be:

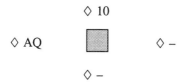

♢ 10

♢ AQ   ♢ –

♢ –

That's better! West has sole guard of the diamond suit and it may now be possible to squeeze him. This technique is known as 'isolating the guard'. In the situation shown above we isolated the diamond guard in the West hand.

On this hand from the 1993 Cap Volmac Pairs, Tony saved himself a guess by using just such a technique:

North/South Game. Dealer West.

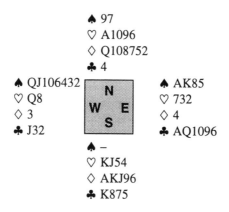

                  ♠ 97
                  ♡ A1096
                  ♢ Q108752
                  ♣ 4

♠ QJ106432   ♠ AK85
♡ Q8   N   ♡ 732
♢ 3   W   E   ♢ 4
♣ J32   S   ♣ AQ1096

                  ♠ –
                  ♡ KJ54
                  ♢ AKJ96
                  ♣ K875

West	North	East	South
	Robson		*Forrester*
3♠	Pass	4♠	Dble
Pass	4NT	5♣	5♢
Pass	6♢	Dble	All Pass

Robson bid 4NT to show at least two playable trump suits. Had Tony held only four diamonds, he would have passed over Five Clubs, allowing his partner to introduce a suit. His actual Five Diamond bid therefore showed at least five diamonds. Trusting from the opponents' bidding that South was very short in spades, Robson was encouraged to bid the slam. An inspired decision.

In response to his partner's lead-directing bid in clubs, West led ♣2. East won with the ace and switched to the spade ace, ruffed by declarer. All depended on picking up the heart queen. How would you have tackled the hand?

If you assume the spades are 7-4, you can gain a complete count on the hand. This reveals that East holds 3 hearts to his partner's 2. So, finessing East for the heart queen gives odds of 3-to-2 in your favour.

Not bad, but it is possible to do better – much better. Look at the club suit. After East has taken his ace, both defenders have it guarded. But if declarer cashes the club king and ruffs a club, this will isolate the club guard in the East hand.

After ruffing the spade ace, Tony drew trumps and ruffed dummy's remaining spade. He then cashed the king of clubs and ruffed a club. Dummy's remaining trumps were run to produce this end position:

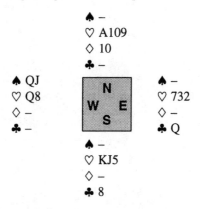

Since East held the sole guard in the club suit, he had to throw a heart on dummy's last trump. The defenders' hearts were now known to be 2-2. Tony discarded the club from his hand and cashed the ace and king of hearts, bringing down the queen.

East was not actually squeezed out of a guard (his ♡732 were valueless in themselves), but he was forced to reveal the location of the heart queen. Such an ending is known as a 'show-up squeeze'. On a day when the sun is shining it can bring you +1540!

When in doubt, run the long suit

Even the best of defenders may find it difficult to keep the right cards if you run your long suit. Many an 'impossible' contract has been landed in this way, including the following Four Spade contract from the Spring Foursomes in 1992.

North/South Game. Dealer West.

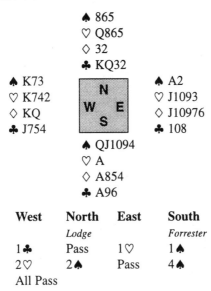

```
              ♠ 865
              ♡ Q865
              ◇ 32
              ♣ KQ32
  ♠ K73          N          ♠ A2
  ♡ K742      W     E       ♡ J1093
  ◇ KQ           S          ◇ J10976
  ♣ J754                    ♣ 108
              ♠ QJ1094
              ♡ A
              ◇ A854
              ♣ A96
```

West	North	East	South
	Lodge		*Forrester*
1♣	Pass	1♡	1♠
2♡	2♠	Pass	4♠
All Pass			

West led a trump and prospects looked bleak indeed after three rounds of trumps had been played. Rather than duck a diamond, which would give the defenders some picture of how that suit lay, Tony cashed two more rounds of trumps immediately. The Grandmaster in the West seat released one heart but found some difficulty with his second discard (his partner had thrown one club and one heart). As it happens, a diamond discard – or even a club – would have beaten the contract. When West chose to throw a second heart Tony cashed the ace of hearts, crossed to a club, and ducked a heart. He now had a total of three heart tricks (!), bringing his total to ten.

The play is known as a pseudo-squeeze. West was not squeezed, in a technical sense, but he 'threw the wrong thing'. Don't dismiss it. If you run your long suit whenever a contract seems hopeless, many an extra trick will come your way.

Watch the entries

When a contract will be cold if the long suit breaks well, start by assuming that it will break poorly. A secondary chance may then emerge – that the defender who guards the long suit also has sole guard of another suit. Suppose, for example, you hold such as ◇ AKQJ3 opposite ◇ 95. Don't be in a hurry to test the suit. The alternative (squeeze) line may require that the diamond entry is left intact. Look at this deal:

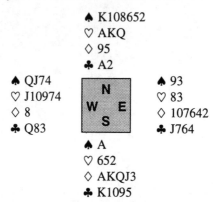

```
                    ♠ K108652
                    ♡ AKQ
                    ◇ 95
                    ♣ A2
   ♠ QJ74          ┌─────────┐      ♠ 93
   ♡ J10974        │   N     │      ♡ 83
   ◇ 8           W │       E │ E    ◇ 107642
   ♣ Q83           │   S     │      ♣ J764
                   └─────────┘
                    ♠ A
                    ♡ 652
                    ◇ AKQJ3
                    ♣ K1095
```

You arrive in 6NT and are pleased to find that you have twelve top tricks unless the diamonds are 5-1 or worse. Very well, in such situations you should start with the assumption that the diamonds do break badly. In that case you might seek a twelfth trick from one of the black suits. Which represents the better prospect, do you think, spades or clubs?

In spades you would need a 3-3 break (or QJ doubleton). A 3-3 break is normally a 36% prospect. Once you assume that the diamonds are 5-1 this in fact drops to around 32%.

How about cashing the club ace and finessing ♣10? This looks better. You will make a twelfth trick from the club suit alone whenever East holds both the queen and jack, or three or fewer cards including one of the honours (♣Jxx, for example). The chance of a third club trick is 52% in fact.

If you test the diamonds at the start it will cost you the contract. Instead you should win the ♡J lead with the ace, cash the ♣A, and finesse ♣10. The play does not gain directly because East's club honour is guarded three times. However, the club guard is now isolated in the East hand. When you cash the ♣K, followed by the major-suit winners, East will be squeezed in the minors. On a different lie of the cards, a spade-diamond squeeze would develop.

The double squeeze

Sometimes you can squeeze both opponents on the same hand. It's not so difficult as you might think, particularly on a deal like this:

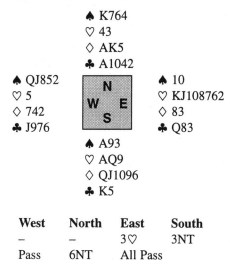

♠ K764
♡ 43
♦ AK5
♣ A1042

♠ QJ852   ♠ 10
♡ 5   ♡ KJ108762
♦ 742   ♦ 83
♣ J976   ♣ Q83

♠ A93
♡ AQ9
♦ QJ1096
♣ K5

West	North	East	South
–	–	3♡	3NT
Pass	6NT	All Pass	

West leads a diamond against 6NT. You win with the ace and play a spade, allowing East's 10 to hold. The purpose of this duck is two-fold: spades may break 3-3 (some hope!), also you have rectified the count for a possible squeeze. West returns the jack of hearts and you finesse the queen successfully. When you cash the ace of spades, East shows out.

If this is new territory for you, the situation may seem bleak. Look at it this way, though: West guards the spades, East guards the hearts, when you run the diamond suit, neither of them will be able to guard the clubs! It's true. Suppose you cash all your winners outside the key club suit. This will be the ending:

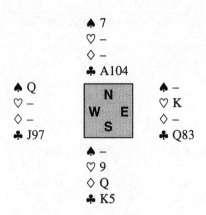

When you play the last diamond, West has to discard a club to retain his spade guard. You throw the now redundant spade threat from dummy and it's East turn to feel the pain. He has to discard a club to retain his heart guard and now you can make three club tricks.

The strip squeeze

One of the most common forms of squeeze is known as the 'strip squeeze', because the play of the squeeze card strips the defender of one of his winners. This is an example of the play:

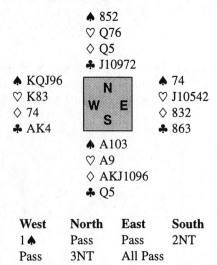

West	North	East	South
1♠	Pass	Pass	2NT
Pass	3NT	All Pass	

West attacks in spades. Declarer can see six diamond tricks and the major-suit aces. How can he bump the total to nine? The answer is surprisingly simple. He wins the second round of spades and runs the diamond suit. Although West has made one trick and has five further winners in his hand, he is powerless to beat the contract. This will be the position with one diamond still to be played:

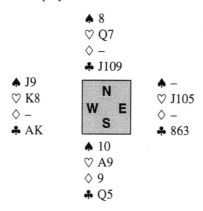

```
              ♠ 8
              ♡ Q7
              ◇ —
              ♣ J109
  ♠ J9        ┌─────────┐        ♠ —
  ♡ K8        │    N    │        ♡ J105
  ◇ —         │ W     E │        ◇ —
  ♣ AK        │    S    │        ♣ 863
              └─────────┘
              ♠ 10
              ♡ A9
              ◇ 9
              ♣ Q5
```

When declarer leads ◇9 West has to retain his guard in hearts. He therefore has to throw another of his winners away. Declarer now puts him in with a spade, forcing him to lead away from the heart king at trick 12.

This was a little bit different from the squeezes we have seen so far. Firstly, the defender was not squeezed out of a guard; he had to discard either a winner or a guard. Secondly, declarer did not have to rectify the count for the squeeze to work. On this particular hand he actually lost three tricks after the squeeze had taken effect.

A defender has no escape when his hand consists solely of winners and a vulnerable holding such as Kx. The situation is different when he also has a losing card with which he can cross to his partner's hand. Suppose you reach this ending:

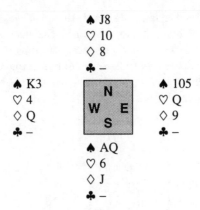

♠ J8
♡ 10
◇ 8
♣ –

♠ K3
♡ 4
◇ Q
♣ –

♠ 105
♡ Q
◇ 9
♣ –

♠ AQ
♡ 6
◇ J
♣ –

No good, is it? Declarer can throw West in with a diamond but he will then be able to exit with the low heart, allowing East to lead a spade through the tenace. The end position was not tight enough. Had declarer lost another trick earlier in the play, rectifying the count by one more trick, West's last three cards would have been ♠K3 and ◇Q. Stripped of his safe exit card, the eventual throw-in would have succeeded.

So, when the key defender had a safe exit card you must squeeze it out of him before you execute the throw-in. Once again the count will have to be rectified – in this case, by losing all the tricks you can afford to lose *except one*. It's a difficult concept which may become clearer if we look at a complete deal.

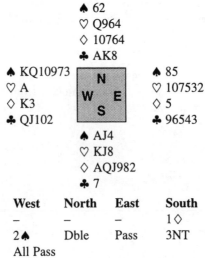

♠ 62
♡ Q964
◇ 10764
♣ AK8

♠ KQ10973
♡ A
◇ K3
♣ QJ102

♠ 85
♡ 107532
◇ 5
♣ 96543

♠ AJ4
♡ KJ8
◇ AQJ982
♣ 7

West	North	East	South
–	–	–	1◇
2♠	Dble	Pass	3NT
All Pass			

A club lead would work well but West starts with the king of spades. Declarer lets this hold and West switches to the queen of clubs. Declarer wins with dummy's ace and leads ◊ 10, playing the 8 from his hand in case he should need a later entry to dummy in the diamond suit. The finesse loses to West's king and he continues with the jack of clubs.

Suppose declarer captures this card and runs the diamond suit. West needs to keep his spade guard (♠Q10) and ♡A. He has space for one more card, however. He will discard ♣10 and keep ♣2, as an entry to his partner's hand. Any attempt at an eventual throw-in will fail. To tighten the end position by one trick, declarer should allow West's jack of clubs to hold at trick 4. When he wins the ♣10 continuation with dummy's king and runs the diamond suit, this will be the ending:

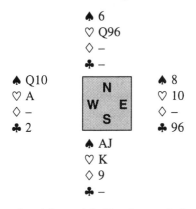

```
              ♠ 6
              ♡ Q96
              ◊ -
              ♣ -
♠ Q10                      ♠ 8
♡ A        N              ♡ 10
◊ -      W   E            ◊ -
♣ 2        S              ♣ 96
              ♠ AJ
              ♡ K
              ◊ 9
              ♣ -
```

West has to throw the club on ◊ 9. You then end-play him with a heart.

You may wonder what would have happened if West had led ♣2 instead of an honour on the first or second round. Declarer could not afford to duck or East would gain the lead and send a spade through. After the club is taken in the dummy, though, West's vulnerable spade tenace would be accompanied by 'all winners'. The strip would work without any further rectification of the count.

The essence of the strip squeeze, then, is a squeeze followed by a throw-in. The defender is squeezed out of one or more winners, then put on lead to concede the extra trick you are seeking.

Here is a final example, this time from the Canadian trials:

Love All. Dealer East.

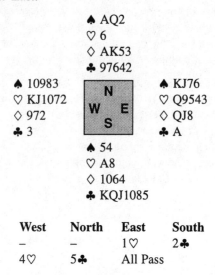

♠ AQ2
♡ 6
◇ AK53
♣ 97642

♠ 10983
♡ KJ1072
◇ 972
♣ 3

♠ KJ76
♡ Q9543
◇ QJ8
♣ A

♠ 54
♡ A8
◇ 1064
♣ KQJ1085

West	North	East	South
–	–	1♡	2♣
4♡	5♣	All Pass	

A heart lead would have given declarer an easy ride but West found the excellent start of ♠ 10. As there was a negligible chance of the spade king being onside, declarer elected to rise with the ace. He eliminated the heart suit and then played a trump. East won with the bare ace and could not safely play a spade or a heart. He exited with the queen of diamonds, won in the dummy, and declarer ran his remaining trumps to reach this ending:

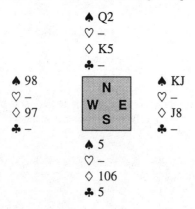

♠ Q2
♡ –
◇ K5
♣ –

♠ 98
♡ –
◇ 97
♣ –

♠ KJ
♡ –
◇ J8
♣ –

♠ 5
♡ –
◇ 106
♣ 5

On the last club declarer threw a spade from dummy. To retain his diamond guard East had to throw a spade winner and he was then thrown in with a spade to lead away from the jack of diamonds.

In this type of end position the defenders may have a chance to fool you. Suppose East had unguarded his jack of diamonds earlier, reducing to: ♠KJ7 and ◊J. As before, he would throw ♠J on the last club. If you were to exit in spades now, placing him with the spade king and two diamonds, you would suffer the annoying spectacle of East cashing a second spade trick.

In practice only the very best of defenders will be able to put you to such a guess. Nine players out of ten will delay their key discard until the last moment. Most of the remainder will drop some clue to the distribution on the way to the end position. Often it is a good idea to watch the intended victim's *partner*, who will tend to signal his distribution accurately to aid the defence. He can be your biggest ally.

Squeeze without the count

Apart from the strip squeeze there are other occasions when it is not practical to rectify the count. If you ducked a trick early on, the opponents might be able to cash you down or perhaps kill a key entry. Look at this deal, for example:

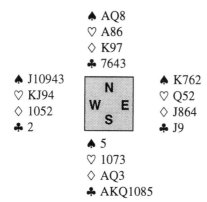

```
              ♠ AQ8
              ♡ A86
              ◊ K97
              ♣ 7643
  ♠ J10943                    ♠ K762
  ♡ KJ94         N            ♡ Q52
  ◊ 1052      W     E         ◊ J864
  ♣ 2            S            ♣ J9
              ♠ 5
              ♡ 1073
              ◊ AQ3
              ♣ AKQ1085
```

South plays in Six Clubs and West leads ♠J. Not difficult to place the top spades, is it? East is a big favourite to hold the king and West is likely to hold J109. You may be surprised to hear that on those two assumptions it is possible to score 12 tricks, provided you read the distribution correctly.

You win the first trick with the ace of spades and cash five rounds of trumps, throwing a heart from dummy. The ace and queen of diamonds come next, leaving South to play:

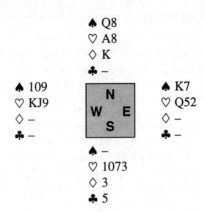

♠ Q8
♡ A8
◇ K
♣ –

♠ 109   ♠ K7
♡ KJ9   ♡ Q52
◇ –   ◇ –
♣ –   ♣ –

♠ –
♡ 1073
◇ 3
♣ 5

When a diamond is led to the king West cannot afford a spade, or a lead of dummy's queen will set up a spade trick. He throws a heart but now East has no good discard. If he throws a heart too, you will continue with ace and another heart, setting up a long heart in the South hand.

Once again a trick was lost after the actual squeeze. Had declarer ducked a heart earlier, the defenders would have played a second heart, removing dummy's ace and killing the squeeze.

8
OUT FOR THE COUNT

In this chapter we will look at 'counting the hand'. Are you still with us, or have you flipped over a few pages, looking for something more interesting? A pity if so, because the expert player spends much of his time at the table in reconstructing the opponents' hands – counting their points, assessing their distribution. It's not a bundle of fun, let's admit it, so why do players bother? Because it brings a huge dividend. If you know where the cards lie, you can play the hand with greater accuracy.

Suppose you are in 7NT on this deal:

```
              ♠ QJ6
              ♡ AKQ
              ◇ K962
              ♣ AQ2
  ♠ 109832                    ♠ 74
  ♡ J97                       ♡ 10854
  ◇ 873                       ◇ J105
  ♣ 83                        ♣ J1095
              ♠ AK5
              ♡ 632
              ◇ AQ4
              ♣ K764
```

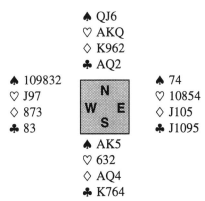

West leads ♠10 and you see that you have three winners in each suit. That's twelve altogether and the extra trick will have to come from one of the minors. An inexperienced player might turn his attention in that direction immediately. Three rounds of clubs would bring no luck, the suit breaking 4-2. The ace and queen of diamonds come next, East producing the jack or 10 on the second round. Declarer will then have to guess whether to finesse dummy's ◇9 on the third round. On the evidence so far gathered, not very much, the odds would favour a finesse of the 9. One down.

A much better idea is to cash the winners in the major suits first. The purpose is twofold. It's possible that a defender will be put to an embarrassing discard. Also, you may gather valuable information on the defenders' distribution.

Suppose you start by cashing three spade tricks. East has to find a discard on the third spade, and if he throws a diamond or a club, your problems will be over. Let's say he guesses well and throws a heart. You now cash three hearts, noting that both defenders follow all the way. Now come the top three clubs, West discarding on the third round.

On this particular deal it was possible to achieve a complete count. West started with five spades, three hearts and two clubs, so the diamonds must be 3-3. The grand slam is made without resort to guesswork.

When Great Britain played Jordan in the 1996 Olympiad, Tony arrived in a vulnerable slam that depended on a queen guess. We say 'guess', but there is nothing a good declarer likes less than guesswork.

Game All. Dealer North.

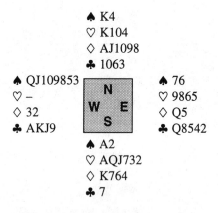

$$\spadesuit\ K4$$
$$\heartsuit\ K104$$
$$\diamondsuit\ AJ1098$$
$$\clubsuit\ 1063$$

$$\spadesuit\ QJ109853$$
$$\heartsuit\ -$$
$$\diamondsuit\ 32$$
$$\clubsuit\ AKJ9$$

$$\spadesuit\ 76$$
$$\heartsuit\ 9865$$
$$\diamondsuit\ Q5$$
$$\clubsuit\ Q8542$$

$$\spadesuit\ A2$$
$$\heartsuit\ AQJ732$$
$$\diamondsuit\ K764$$
$$\clubsuit\ 7$$

West	North	East	South
Ghanem	*Robson*	*Ghanem*	*Forrester*
–	1♢	Pass	2♡
4♠	Pass	Pass	6♢
Dble	6♡	All Pass	

The Westerly Ghanem brother doubled Six Diamonds, a Lightner double that requested a heart lead. Andy Robson smartly corrected the contract to Six Hearts and West launched the defence with the king and ace of clubs.

Tony ruffed the second round and drew trumps, East showing up with all four. All now depended on the diamond guess. Tony cashed two rounds of spades, both defenders following, and ruffed dummy's last club, West producing a deceptive jack.

It is at this stage that many a declarer would scratch his head, trying desperately to remember what length signal in clubs East had given at trick 1. When the auction has been dramatic it is all too easy to let your attention drop for a few seconds in the early stages of the play. Tony had noted East's 2, however. It was reasonable to place West with seven spades for his Four Spade bid, so his distribution was likely to be 7-0-2-4. The king and ace of diamonds duly dropped the queen from East and that was +1430.

Sometimes you must take special steps to gain a count. Tony played this 6NT contract during the 1984 Camrose trials:

North/South Game. Dealer East.

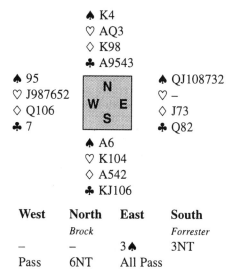

```
              ♠ K4
              ♡ AQ3
              ◇ K98
              ♣ A9543
  ♠ 95                        ♠ QJ108732
  ♡ J987652      N            ♡ –
  ◇ Q106      W     E         ◇ J73
  ♣ 7            S            ♣ Q82
              ♠ A6
              ♡ K104
              ◇ A542
              ♣ KJ106
```

West	North	East	South
	Brock		*Forrester*
–	–	3♠	3NT
Pass	6NT	All Pass	

West led ♠9, declarer winning with the ace. At this stage East's length in spades made West the favourite to hold the queen of clubs. There was no need to take an immediate view in the club suit, however. By playing on the red suits, further information could be brought to the surface. At trick 2 Tony ducked a diamond. He won the spade return and cashed the ace of hearts, East showing out, followed by a diamond to the king.

Since East held at most seven spades and four diamonds alongside his heart void, he was marked with at least two clubs. Tony next cashed the ace of clubs in case the clubs were 4-0 (in that case dummy's ◊ K and ♡ Q would be needed to resolve the blockage in clubs). West followed to the first club and it was now safe to cash the king of diamonds. When all followed, the count was complete. Tony played a club to the jack, knowing the finesse would succeed, and claimed the remainder.

It's an important theme, seeking the distribution of the opponents' hands. The following deal was played carelessly:

Love All. Dealer South.

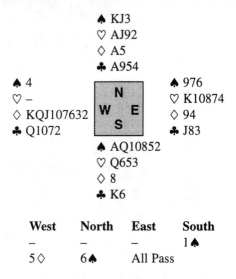

♠ KJ3
♡ AJ92
◊ A5
♣ A954

♠ 4
♡ –
◊ KQJ107632
♣ Q1072

♠ 976
♡ K10874
◊ 94
♣ J83

♠ AQ10852
♡ Q653
◊ 8
♣ K6

West	North	East	South
–	–	–	1♠
5◊	6♠	All Pass	

Declarer won the diamond king lead with the ace and drew trumps in three rounds. When a heart was led towards dummy, West showed out. The jack of hearts was played, losing to the king, and East returned a diamond. Declarer ruffed in the South hand, cashed two clubs, and ruffed a club. He then ran his remaining trumps, hoping to catch East in a heart-club squeeze. Unfortunately, it was West who held the club guard and the slam went one down.

Declarer may have cursed his luck but in fact luck had little to do with it. After drawing trumps, he should have ruffed a diamond in his hand. East would follow suit, giving him at least 5 cards in spades and diamonds. When West then showed void on the first round of hearts, East would be known to hold at least 10 cards outside clubs. He could not therefore hold 4 clubs! With the proposed squeeze doomed to failure, another line of play might have come into focus. Can you spot it?

You should rise with the ace on the first round of hearts. You can then cash two clubs, and ruff a club. These cards would remain:

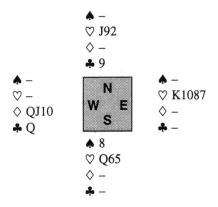

♠ —
♡ J92
♢ —
♣ 9

♠ —   ♠ —
♡ —   ♡ K1087
♢ QJ10   ♢ —
♣ Q   ♣ —

♠ 8
♡ Q65
♢ —
♣ —

East will not enjoy your next move, a heart to the jack. After winning with the king, he will have to lead from ♡ 10. The simple step of ruffing a diamond enables you to obtain a full picture of the distribution.

Law of Vacant Places

On many deals you can gather only a partial count on the defenders' cards. Suppose you discover, for example, that East has 2 clubs to his partner's 6. East will then hold 11 non-clubs to his partner's 7 and it would be fair to conclude that East was an '11-to-7 on' favourite to hold a missing queen in one of the other suits. That is the situation here:

North/South Game. Dealer South.

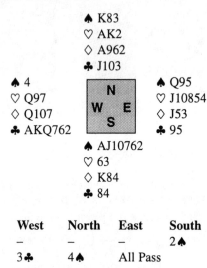

```
                    ♠ K83
                    ♡ AK2
                    ◇ A962
                    ♣ J103
     ♠ 4                         ♠ Q95
     ♡ Q97          N            ♡ J10854
     ◇ Q107      W     E         ◇ J53
     ♣ AKQ762       S            ♣ 95
                    ♠ AJ10762
                    ♡ 63
                    ◇ K84
                    ♣ 84
```

West	North	East	South
–	–	–	2♠
3♣	4♠	All Pass	

You open with a Weak Two and arrive in Four Spades. West starts with the three top clubs and you ruff the third round. You now need to pick up the trump suit. Although you have little idea how the red suits lie, you do know that East started with 11 'non-clubs' and West with only 7. You cross to the trump king, two small cards appearing, and lead a second round, East playing the 9. It's no certainty but you should finesse the jack now. East has 9 vacant places in his hand which may contain the trump queen; West has only 6. The chance that East holds the missing queen is therefore 9 in 15 (60%).

This style of reasoning is known as the 'Law of Vacant Places'. At the key moment West had 6 unknown cards in his hand, East had 9. This tilted the 'normal' odds. Note also that declarer was unable to play on the red suits with safety, otherwise he could have found out West's exact distribution.

When the contract is in no-trumps, it is possible to mis-apply this Law and draw a false conclusion:

Love All. Dealer South.

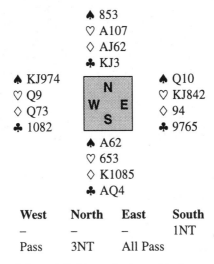

                    ♠ 853
                    ♡ A107
                    ◊ AJ62
                    ♣ KJ3
    ♠ KJ974   ♠ Q10
    ♡ Q9   ♡ KJ842
    ◊ Q73   ◊ 94
    ♣ 1082   ♣ 9765
                    ♠ A62
                    ♡ 653
                    ◊ K1085
                    ♣ AQ4

West	North	East	South
–	–	–	1NT
Pass	3NT	All Pass	

West leads a fourth-best ♠7, East winning with the queen and returning ♠10. West overtakes with the jack and clears the suit, East throwing a heart. Everything depends on your guess in the diamond suit. It is tempting to think: West held 5 spades to his partner's 2; with 11 vacant places to his partner's 8, East is therefore favourite to hold the queen of diamonds. Do you see any fallacy in this reasoning?

Suppose North had been the dealer. He would have opened 1NT, raised to 3NT, and East would have led ♡4. When East turned up with five hearts to his partner's two, the same reasoning as above would lead to the conclusion that West was favourite to hold the diamond queen!

Since players normally lead their longest suit against no-trumps, no conclusion should be drawn from the relative lengths in that particular suit unless the difference is significant. The situation is roughly this – if a player leads from a 4-card suit, he will be an initial favourite to hold any missing card in another suit. If he leads from a 5-card suit, the odds will be roughly level. If he has a suit of 6 cards or more, his partner will be favourite to hold any missing card.

Information on the defenders' suit lengths comes from various sources. How many occur to you? Any bids they have made will certainly help. The most concrete evidence, of course, comes when they actually show out of a suit. There is one other major source of information, their signals!

It is becoming increasingly popular for defenders to make distributional signals as they follow to each suit. On many hands these will greatly aid the defence. To redress the balance, you must take full advantage of them yourself, as declarer. Suppose you have to play 8 boards against a pair in some Swiss event. Don't take a small snooze the first time partner has to play a hand. Watch closely to see whether the defenders are signalling their suit lengths. You may be glad of this knowledge when you have to play a close game on the next hand. Also, don't ask too many questions on their signalling methods. You want them to play 'true' cards; if you show too much interest they may false-card to fool you.

Counting the defenders' points

So far we have concentrated on counting distribution. On this deal played by Tony in the 1995 Premier League that technique alone would have led to the wrong answer.

East/West Game. Dealer West.

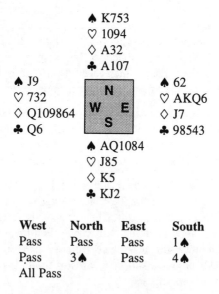

```
                    ♠ K753
                    ♡ 1094
                    ◇ A32
                    ♣ A107
    ♠ J9              N            ♠ 62
    ♡ 732        W       E         ♡ AKQ6
    ◇ Q109864        S            ◇ J7
    ♣ Q6                          ♣ 98543
                    ♠ AQ1084
                    ♡ J85
                    ◇ K5
                    ♣ KJ2
```

West	North	East	South
Pass	Pass	Pass	1♠
Pass	3♠	Pass	4♠
All Pass			

A diamond or trump opening lead would have allowed an easy elimination (draw trumps, eliminate the diamonds, and exit in hearts). West found the only safe lead of a heart and East cashed three winners in the suit, switching to a trump.

Trumps were 2-2 and Tony now needed to pick up the queen of clubs. It was natural to seek extra information by playing three rounds of diamonds. This revealed that East had started with a jack doubleton. If you were relying only on a count of the distribution you would now conclude that East held at least five clubs and was therefore a strong favourite to hold the queen of the suit. However, suppose that East had been dealt:

♠ 62
♡ AKQ6
♢ J7
♣ Q8543

He would surely have opened the bidding! This piece of evidence could not be ignored. Tony duly played king and another club, picking up West's queen and making the contract.

Canadian star, Fred Gitelman, used similar reasoning to net a top score on this deal from the pairs championship in the 1995 Montreal Regional.

Love All. Dealer West.

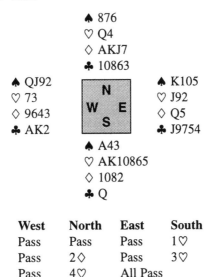

```
              ♠ 876
              ♡ Q4
              ♢ AKJ7
              ♣ 10863
  ♠ QJ92                      ♠ K105
  ♡ 73          N            ♡ J92
  ♢ 9643      W   E          ♢ Q5
  ♣ AK2         S            ♣ J9754
              ♠ A43
              ♡ AK10865
              ♢ 1082
              ♣ Q
```

West	North	East	South
Pass	Pass	Pass	1♡
Pass	2♢	Pass	3♡
Pass	4♡	All Pass	

West led the king of clubs against Gitelman's Four Hearts, East showing an odd number of cards in the suit and South dropping the queen. West now switched to the queen of spades, allowed to win, and a low spade to East's king and declarer's ace. There was some chance of a trump coup, should East hold ♡Jxxx, so Gitelman continued with the ace of trumps and a trump to the queen, both defenders following. A club ruff in the South hand allowed declarer to draw the last trump. He now needed to score three diamond tricks without conceding a trick in the suit. How should the diamonds be played, do you think?

Gitelman recalled that West had failed to open the bidding but had already shown up with ♠QJ and ♣AK. With a 12-count West would doubtless have opened the bidding, so the only hope was that East held a singleton or doubleton queen of diamonds.

Having reached this conclusion, many declarers would bash out the diamond ace-king, triumphantly claiming ten tricks when East's queen fell. Gitelman went the extra mile. He unblocked the 10 and 8 of diamonds under dummy's honours! When East's queen fell he crossed to his hand with another club ruff and finessed dummy's ◇7. A precious overtrick was the outcome.

Counting points was the answer on this hand too, played against Mexico in the 1980 Olympiad:

North/South Game. Dealer West.

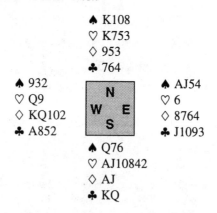

```
              ♠ K108
              ♡ K753
              ◇ 953
              ♣ 764
  ♠ 932                    ♠ AJ54
  ♡ Q9          N          ♡ 6
  ◇ KQ102    W   E         ◇ 8764
  ♣ A852        S          ♣ J1093
              ♠ Q76
              ♡ AJ10842
              ◇ AJ
              ♣ KQ
```

West	North	East	South
	Smolski		*Forrester*
Pass	Pass	Pass	1♡
Pass	2♡	Pass	4♡
All Pass			

The Mexican West led the diamond king, taken by the ace. Tony drew trumps in two rounds and advanced the king of clubs. West captured and played queen and another diamond, declarer ruffing. After cashing the queen of clubs, Tony crossed to ♡7 and ruffed dummy's last club. These cards remained:

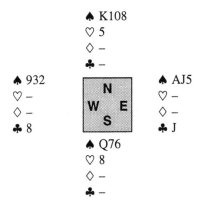

Since West had shown 11 points already and had not opened the bidding, it was likely that East held the jack of spades as well as the ace. Tony played a spade and called for dummy's king. East won with the ace but then had to lead away from his jack (or concede a ruff-and-discard). That was +620.

The defence was not as tight as it might have been. There were insufficient entries to dummy for declarer to eliminate the minors under his own steam. Had West exited in clubs, rather than forcing declarer with a third diamond, the contract would have failed.

9
CONFIDENCE TRICKS

Some declarers are easy to defend against. They play the dummy in straightforward fashion, giving no thought to deception. Other declarers are altogether more cunning. They give consideration to every card they play, putting you to a guess time and time again. This is a simple example of the difference between the two styles. South is in Six Spades, say, and the heart suit lies like this:

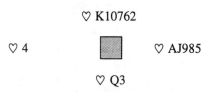

♡ K10762

♡ 4　　　　　♡ AJ985

♡ Q3

West leads 4 to his partner's ace. Mr Straightforward will follow with the 3, making it obvious to East that the lead is a singleton. Mr Cunning will contribute the queen, leaving open in East's eyes the possibility that the lead is from a doubleton. East will still return a heart most of the time, but now and again he will switch his attention elsewhere.

Suppose that you are in a major-suit slam and the unbid diamond suit lies like this:

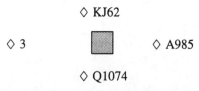

◇ KJ62

◇ 3　　　　　◇ A985

◇ Q1074

West has led the lowest outstanding spot-card this time, so the only chance is to persuade East that his partner is leading from length. Any ideas?

You must conjure the image in East's eyes that the opening lead is from such as ◇ Q1043. Call for dummy's jack and contribute the 7 from your hand. If East gives you a weary smile and returns a diamond, at least you will have tried your best.

Scrambling the defenders' signals

On the examples in the previous section we were trying to fool the player in the third seat, to dissuade him from reading partner's lead as a singleton. Just as often, the object will be to deceive the defender on lead, to encourage or discourage a continuation of the suit led.

Suppose you are in a major-suit game and West leads ◇ A in this lay-out:

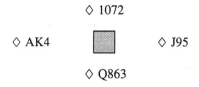

◇ 1072

◇ AK4   ◇ J95

◇ Q863

If East is using standard signals (high to encourage, low to discourage) he will play the 5, warning his partner against a continuation. Since you want West to cash his second high diamond, you must try to make East's 5 look like an encouraging card. Which card would you play from hand, the 8? That's no good. West will reason that if East held ◇ Q653 he would have signalled with the 6. He will know, therefore, that your 8 is a false card. The right card is the 6. You cover East's spot-card as cheaply as possible. West may now conclude that his partner holds ◇ Q53.

This is the opposite case, when you may not want West to continue:

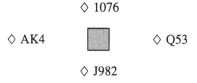

◇ 1076

◇ AK4   ◇ Q53

◇ J982

West leads ◇ A and East encourages with the 5. No benefit will come from random 'clever' cards such as the 8 or 9. When the 2 does not appear, West will be all the more likely to read East's 5 as encouraging. Your only chance is to play the 2, leaving open the possibility that East started with J95 or J85.

These false cards lose effectiveness if you have to consult the ceiling to work out what to do. The basic rule is not hard to remember: to encourage a continuation you play high, covering East's spot card; to discourage a continuation, play low.

When the defenders are playing 'reverse signals' (low to encourage, high to discourage), declarer must follow the same scheme: low to encourage a continuation, cover East's card to discourage:

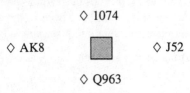

$\diamondsuit$ 1074

$\diamondsuit$ AK8 $\diamondsuit$ J52

$\diamondsuit$ Q963

West leads the ace and East (playing reverse signals) discourages with the 5. To encourage a continuation you must play the 3. It is now possible in West's eyes that East has encouraged from Q95 or Q65.

Feigning weakness

In no-trump contracts the defenders will sometimes attack in a suit that you hold strongly. You must encourage them in this abortive venture. Declarer was not up to the task here:

Love All. Dealer South.

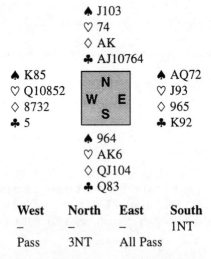

	♠ J103	
	♡ 74	
	◇ AK	
	♣ AJ10764	

♠ K85		♠ AQ72
♡ Q10852		♡ J93
◇ 8732		◇ 965
♣ 5		♣ K92

	♠ 964	
	♡ AK6	
	◇ QJ104	
	♣ Q83	

West	North	East	South
–	–	–	1NT
Pass	3NT	All Pass	

West led ♡5, East producing the jack. Declarer won with the ace and ran the queen of clubs, losing to the king. All now depended on East's next move. It seemed to him that if South had started with three hearts to the ace he would have held up the ace of hearts for a couple of rounds. Surely

South must hold the king of hearts as well as the ace, and in that case he would have nine tricks on a heart return. East switched to a low spade, with gratifying results.

Do you see how declarer might have done better? Suppose he wins the first round of hearts with the king. Now East can make no such deduction from the fact that declarer did not hold up; with ♡ Kxx, he would have no option but to win. (Expert defenders might still get it right. East should duck the first round of clubs, hoping for a helpful discard from partner on the next round. Since West knows a heart continuation will not beat the contract, he should throw a spectacular ♡ Q on the next club. It will then be clear to East that a spade switch is the only chance.)

West attacked South's stronghold on the following 3NT contract, played by Tony in the 1990 Staten Bank tournament in the Hague. Once again it was in declarer's interest to disguise this fact.

East/West Game. Dealer South.

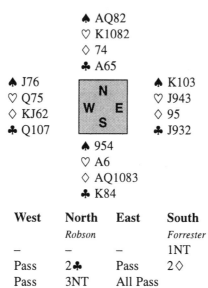

```
                    ♠ AQ82
                    ♡ K1082
                    ◇ 74
                    ♣ A65
        ♠ J76          N          ♠ K103
        ♡ Q75                     ♡ J943
        ◇ KJ62      W   E         ◇ 95
        ♣ Q107         S          ♣ J932
                    ♠ 954
                    ♡ A6
                    ◇ AQ1083
                    ♣ K84
```

West	North	East	South
	Robson		*Forrester*
–	–	–	1NT
Pass	2♣	Pass	2◇
Pass	3NT	All Pass	

West started with ◇ 2, the 9 appearing from East. The king and jack of diamonds were known to be with West. Declarer could win the first diamond trick with the 10 and eventually build a third trick from the diamond suit. But that would bring the total to only eight, with prospects of a ninth trick uncertain. How much better if he could make *four* diamond tricks!

At trick one Tony captured East's ◊9 with the queen and immediately returned ◊3. West, who had no wish to open a new suit from his side of the table, allowed the second round of diamonds to run to his partner's 10. Or so he thought … Dummy's 7 won the trick and Tony could now cross to his hand and play ace and another diamond. That was nine tricks.

Feigning strength

On the next deal, from the semi-final of the 1988 Gold Cup, Tony illustrated the matching technique – feigning strength in a suit that is poorly held:

Love All. Dealer South.

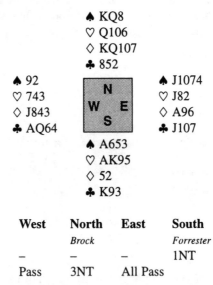

```
                    ♠ KQ8
                    ♡ Q106
                    ◊ KQ107
                    ♣ 852
    ♠ 92                          ♠ J1074
    ♡ 743            N            ♡ J82
    ◊ J843       W     E          ◊ A96
    ♣ AQ64           S            ♣ J107
                    ♠ A653
                    ♡ AK95
                    ◊ 52
                    ♣ K93
```

West	North	East	South
	Brock		*Forrester*
–	–	–	1NT
Pass	3NT	All Pass	

West led ♡4 to the 6, 8 and 9. Tony played a diamond to the king and this card won. Suppose you have been playing the hand. What would you have done next?

Some players would be tempted to bolt for home, playing on spades in the hope that the suit would break 3-3. Others would return to hand with a heart and play a second diamond, hoping that West held the ace. Tony tried something different, a club to the 9! On the face of it, it was a dangerous play; the defenders might have cashed four clubs and the diamond ace when either of the other two lines would have yielded nine easy tricks.

What did happen? West won with the queen of clubs and played another heart, taken by declarer's ace. Now Tony played a second round of diamonds, calling for dummy's 10 when West played low. East won with the ace and, deceived by Tony's early play in clubs, returned another heart. Declarer now had nine tricks. (Had East returned ♣J, Tony would have had to guess to cover, blocking the suit).

East could have done better, of course, by rising with the jack of clubs on the first round. A defender is unlikely to do this in a suit that declarer has chosen to play. Indeed, the chance of a defensive blockage contributed to Tony's decision that the risk of playing on clubs was worthwhile.

The next deal arose in a pairs tournament (a Grand Prix heat in Dunblane, Scotland). The moment the dummy went down, Tony realised he was not in the best contract. Something special would be needed to achieve a good pairs score.

North/South Game. Dealer North.

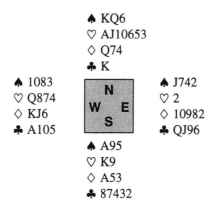

                    ♠ KQ6
                    ♡ AJ10653
                    ◇ Q74
                    ♣ K

    ♠ 1083   ♠ J742
    ♡ Q874   N   ♡ 2
    ◇ KJ6   W   E   ◇ 10982
    ♣ A105   S   ♣ QJ96

                    ♠ A95
                    ♡ K9
                    ◇ A53
                    ♣ 87432

West	North	East	South
	Robson		*Forrester*
–	1♡	Pass	1NT
Pass	2NT	Pass	3NT
All Pass			

North-South were playing a strong club system. Tony's 1NT response was forcing and partner's 2NT rebid showed around 14-15 points and a 6-card heart suit. West led ♠3, taken by dummy's king. Remembering that it is pairs, how would you have continued?

At trick 2 Tony led the king of clubs! Whenever the ace and queen of clubs were split it was possible that the defender would hold off the ace, expecting clubs to be South's strong suit. West did indeed hold off the ace. Tony continued with a heart to the 9, finessing towards the defender who was less likely to play on clubs. West won with the queen (not the best) and continued with another spade. Now Tony had his +430, beating the pairs in hearts who collected only +420. The idea was the same as in the previous deal – feigning strength at your point of weakness.

Use your imagination!

Suppose you have to play a trump suit of AQ76542 opposite a void. Would you play the ace first or a low card? Tony faced just such a situation on this deal from the European Pairs Final in 1985:

North/South Game. Dealer East.

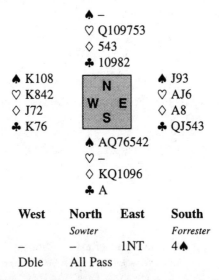

West	North	East	South
	Sowter		*Forrester*
–	–	1NT	4♠
Dble	All Pass		

West led ♡2, East covering dummy's 9 with the jack. Tony ruffed and promptly led the *queen* of trumps!

West gave this card a good look, you can imagine. From his point of view it was possible that declarer held eight trumps to the queen-jack. In that case it might cost a trick to win with the king; the second round could then be ducked to East's bare ace. West eventually played low on the trump queen and did not look too well when this card held the trick. Tony continued with ace and another trump, making the contract despite the loss of two diamond tricks.

Tony's play of the trump queen would cost only when East had started with king doubleton in trumps. It was likely to gain whenever West held three or four trumps to the king. West would probably duck even with such as KJ8x (fearing that declarer held Q109 to seven).

Tempting a cover

Suppose you are in 3NT and West leads ♣2, the suit lying like this:

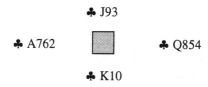

If East can be persuaded to part with his queen, you will score two tricks in the suit. In such situations you should put your juiciest maggot on the hook. Call for dummy's jack. (A good defender may still not cover. He will reason that if you held ace doubleton you would surely have played the 9 from dummy.)

Now the contract is Six Hearts and this is your trump suit:

The odds marginally favour playing for the drop and many players would simply bang out the ace. Better in the long run is to cross to dummy and lead the queen. It's surprising how many defenders will cover from Kx. If no cover comes, play ♡A as before.

The same idea may be successful in this situation:

If East covers the queen, he will not be the first (or last) to fall for the trap. It is poor defence to cover, of course, since if South held such as ◇ AJ64 his normal play would be a low card to the jack.

Sometimes you are faced with two possible ways of making a contract, one involving a finesse against a king. By presenting the queen of that suit early on, tempting a cover, you may be able to combine the two chances. The ploy was used successfully on this deal:

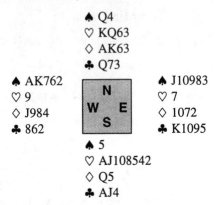

```
              ♠ Q4
              ♡ KQ63
              ◇ AK63
              ♣ Q73
  ♠ AK762                    ♠ J10983
  ♡ 9          N             ♡ 7
  ◇ J984     W   E           ◇ 1072
  ♣ 862        S             ♣ K1095
              ♠ 5
              ♡ AJ108542
              ◇ Q5
              ♣ AJ4
```

West led the ace and king of spades against Six Hearts, declarer ruffing the second round. There were eleven top tricks and two roughly equal chances of a twelfth. If East held the king of clubs a simple finesse would succeed. Alternatively, declarer could run the heart suit, hoping that the king of clubs lay in the same hand as the long diamonds.

There was a fair prospect of enjoying both these chances. After ruffing the second spade, declarer crossed to dummy with a trump and led the queen of clubs. There may be a few players around who would duck smoothly in the East seat. We have not met many of them! East did in fact cover and declarer claimed the remainder. Had East played low, declarer would have risen with the ace and run the hearts, playing for the alternative chance of the minor-suit squeeze.

Tony followed a similar line of play on this deal from the 1994 Life Master Pairs in the USA.

East/West Game, Dealer South.

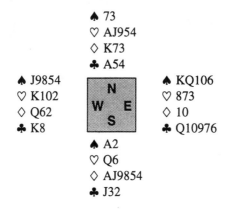

North (Andersen):
♠ 73
♡ AJ954
◇ K73
♣ A54

West:
♠ J9854
♡ K102
◇ Q62
♣ K8

East:
♠ KQ106
♡ 873
◇ 10
♣ Q10976

South (Forrester):
♠ A2
♡ Q6
◇ AJ9854
♣ J32

West	North	East	South
	Andersen		*Forrester*
–	–	–	1NT
Pass	2◇	Pass	2♡
Pass	3NT	All Pass	

West led ♠5 to East's queen and Tony won with the ace. The main chance of nine tricks lay in the diamond suit. Suppose declarer starts by playing the king and ace of diamonds. With the entries to the South hand exhausted, it will no longer be possible to take advantage of a favourable heart position; West will cover ♡Q, stranding declarer in the dummy.

At trick 2 Tony advanced the queen of hearts! The bidding had not revealed South's six-card diamond suit and West can hardly be blamed for covering with the king. Tony won the trick with dummy's ace and continued with the king and ace of diamonds, finding that West had the suit stopped. But now he could take advantage of the favourable lie in the heart suit. A finesse of ♡9 succeeded and when the suit proved to be 3-3 the game was made. Had the king of hearts not appeared from West, Tony would have called for dummy's ace and relied on the diamonds coming in.

10
AVOIDANCE PLAY

It often happens, particularly in no-trump contracts, that you can afford one defender to gain the lead but not the other. Suppose you are in 3NT and West leads the king of spades in this layout:

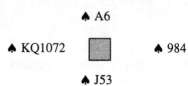

♠ A6

♠ KQ1072   ♠ 984

♠ J53

You win with dummy's ace and must then attempt to develop nine tricks without letting East, the 'danger hand', into the lead. If, for example, you needed three diamond tricks from AJxx in the dummy opposite K109x in your hand, you would take the diamond finesse towards West, the 'safe hand'. Even if the finesse lost, West would not be able to continue spades profitably.

This is the basic idea behind the technique known as Avoidance Play. You develop the tricks you need without allowing the dangerous defender to gain the lead.

Declarer had to protect his spade holding on this Four Heart contract:

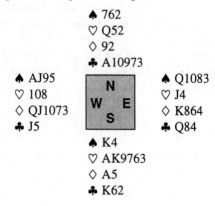

♠ 762
♥ Q52
♦ 92
♣ A10973

♠ AJ95   ♠ Q1083
♥ 108   ♥ J4
♦ QJ1073   ♦ K864
♣ J5   ♣ Q84

♠ K4
♥ AK9763
♦ A5
♣ K62

West led the queen of diamonds and declarer allowed this to hold, preventing West from crossing to East's king later in the play. (If East had overtaken the queen with the king declarer would have captured immediately, trusting that dummy's ◇ 9 would block the defenders' communications.)

Declarer won the diamond continuation and cashed the ace and king of trumps. When the suit broke 2-2, he crossed to the ace of clubs and ran ♣ 10 into the safe hand. West now had to cash the spade ace to prevent an overtrick. Had the trumps broken 3-1, declarer would have drawn a third round with dummy's queen; he would have then run ♣ 10 on the first round of the suit. The deal illustrates the two main techniques for freezing a defender out of the play – the hold-up, and the finesse into the safe hand.

A different technique was required on this deal from the 1996 Jersey Congress:

Game All. Dealer West.

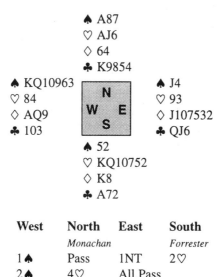

```
                    ♠ A87
                    ♡ AJ6
                    ◇ 64
                    ♣ K9854
    ♠ KQ10963                    ♠ J4
    ♡ 84          N              ♡ 93
    ◇ AQ9      W     E           ◇ J107532
    ♣ 103         S              ♣ QJ6
                    ♠ 52
                    ♡ KQ10752
                    ◇ K8
                    ♣ A72
```

West	North	East	South
	Monachan		*Forrester*
1♠	Pass	1NT	2♡
2♠	4♡	All Pass	

A low spade lead would have beaten the contract but West made the natural start of the king of spades. Tony allowed this card to hold, preventing a subsequent spade entry to the East hand. He won the spade continuation in the dummy and drew trumps in two rounds with the king and ace. Declarer now needed to set up the clubs without allowing East on lead.

One possibility was to play ace, king and another club, winning if West held three clubs, or such as QJ doubleton (the second round would be ducked). Another chance was to lead the first round of clubs towards the king, then duck the second round unless the queen appeared from East. This would win when West held Qx or various 3-card holdings.

A much better play was available. The bidding, and the fall of East's ♠J on the second round, suggested that West had started with six spades. Tony therefore cashed the ace and king of clubs and exited with a spade, discarding his last club. West had no safe card to play. Nor could West have played the last club, had he held that card. The club suit would then be established and declarer could reach dummy with a trump.

Suppose East had held three trumps to West's one, his shape being 2-3-5-3. There would then be an interesting defensive point. Declarer would lead a third round of spades immediately after the king and ace of trumps (aiming to discard a club, ruff the clubs good, and return to dummy with ♡J). To beat the contract East would have to ruff the third spade! Forced to overruff, declarer would have no way to set up the clubs without allowing East on lead.

Strangely, allowing the opening lead to win can pay dividends *even when you have no loser in the suit*. By swapping one loser for another, you may be able to keep the dangerous defender off lead. That's what happened here:

East/West Game. Dealer West.

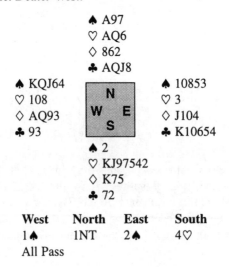

```
                    ♠ A97
                    ♡ AQ6
                    ◇ 862
                    ♣ AQJ8
    ♠ KQJ64                        ♠ 10853
    ♡ 108            N             ♡ 3
    ◇ AQ93       W     E           ◇ J104
    ♣ 93            S              ♣ K10654
                    ♠ 2
                    ♡ KJ97542
                    ◇ K75
                    ♣ 72
```

West	North	East	South
1♠	1NT	2♠	4♡
All Pass			

A club lead would have beaten the contract but West looked no further than the spade king. Declarer had nine top winners and needed to develop the game-going trick from the club suit without East gaining the lead. This could be done by ducking the king of spades lead. When West switched to a club declarer rose with the ace, drew trumps with the king and ace, and discarded his remaining club on the ace of spades. He could then lead the queen of clubs, planning to discard a diamond if the queen was not covered. The contract was secure whoever held the king of clubs.

Tony used a similar play on this deal from the quarter-finals of the 1994 Vanderbilt:

Dealer South. Love All.

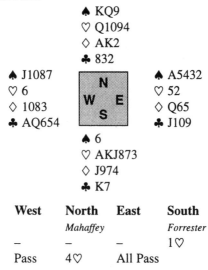

<pre>
              ♠ KQ9
              ♡ Q1094
              ◇ AK2
              ♣ 832
  ♠ J1087   ♠ A5432
  ♡ 6   N   ♡ 52
  ◇ 1083   W   E   ◇ Q65
  ♣ AQ654   S   ♣ J109
              ♠ 6
              ♡ AKJ873
              ◇ J974
              ♣ K7
</pre>

West	North	East	South
	Mahaffey		*Forrester*
–	–	–	1♡
Pass	4♡	All Pass	

West led the jack of spades against Four Hearts. You can see what would happen if declarer covers in the dummy. East would win and switch to clubs, the defenders claiming two tricks there. With no way to avoid a subsequent loser in diamonds, that would be one down.

Tony ducked the spade lead in dummy. This was an example of the 'classic' form of avoidance play – East could still gain the lead, by overtaking partner's jack with the ace, but he would have to pay an unacceptably high price. He would set up two spade winners in dummy, good for two diamond discards.

At the table East did overtake with the ace and switch to a club (the right defence had declarer held ♣Kxx). Ten tricks resulted. East would have done no better by playing low. After drawing trumps, declarer would lead the spade king from dummy, setting up a discard for one of his clubs. The only losers would be ♠J, a diamond and a club.

Another valuable technique is that of leading towards an honour, prepared to duck if a high card appears from the safe hand. Australian international, Margi Bourke, used the idea on this deal:

Love All. Dealer West.

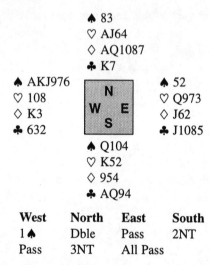

```
                    ♠ 83
                    ♡ AJ64
                    ◇ AQ1087
                    ♣ K7
   ♠ AKJ976                        ♠ 52
   ♡ 108          ┌─────────┐      ♡ Q973
   ◇ K3           │    N    │      ◇ J62
   ♣ 632          │  W   E  │      ♣ J1085
                  │    S    │
                  └─────────┘
                    ♠ Q104
                    ♡ K52
                    ◇ 954
                    ♣ AQ94
```

West	North	East	South
1♠	Dble	Pass	2NT
Pass	3NT	All Pass	

West would have done best to lead a low spade; the defenders could then have cashed their spade tricks whichever of them gained the lead. West, however, decided to cash the ace of spades at trick 1. He then switched to a club, East's 10 drawing South's queen. Bourke needed to develop the diamond suit without East gaining the lead. At trick 3 she led a diamond towards dummy. It would not help West to put in the king, as declarer would allow the card to hold. He in fact played low and dummy's queen was finessed successfully.

To play the ace of diamonds next would cost the contract; East would win the third round of diamonds with the jack and fire a spade through. Declarer's plan was to cross to the king of hearts and lead a second diamond towards the dummy, but she had to be careful to score her three club honours. Bourke cashed the king of clubs, crossed to the heart king, and cashed the ace of clubs. Only then did she lead a second diamond. The king appeared from West and declarer played low in the dummy.

Whatever West returned, declarer could now score four diamonds, three clubs and two hearts. (Had West's shape been 6-3-2-2, he could have pitched ◇K when the third club was cashed, but this risk was unavoidable.)

The theme was the same on this deal, played by Tony in the 1993 Life Master Pairs in the USA. Again it was that villain, East, who had to be kept out of the lead.

North/South Game. Dealer South.

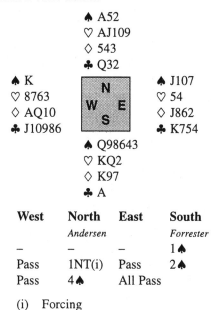

<pre>
                    ♠ A52
                    ♡ AJ109
                    ◇ 543
                    ♣ Q32
    ♠ K   ♠ J107
    ♡ 8763   N   ♡ 54
    ◇ AQ10   W   E   ◇ J862
    ♣ J10986   S   ♣ K754
                    ♠ Q98643
                    ♡ KQ2
                    ◇ K97
                    ♣ A
</pre>

West	North	East	South
	Andersen		*Forrester*
–	–	–	1♠
Pass	1NT(i)	Pass	2♠
Pass	4♠	All Pass	

(i)   Forcing

West led the jack of clubs, won by the ace. Five trumps, four hearts, and the club ace would bring the total to ten. But if East gained the lead in trumps a diamond switch would put the contract in danger. At trick 2 Tony led a trump from the South hand. When the king appeared from West, he ducked in the dummy. It was a simple yet masterly play. After ruffing the club continuation, he was able to draw trumps without East gaining the lead. A diamond was thrown on dummy's long heart and that was ten tricks.

Had declarer won West's king of trumps with the ace the contract would have failed. East would have ruffed the third round of hearts and switched to the *jack* of diamonds, collecting three diamond tricks for the defence.

One of the most common forms of avoidance play involves no more than leading a low card through a defender's honour. Look at this club position, for example:

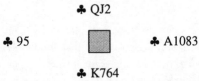

♣ QJ2

♣ 95 ⬜ ♣ A1083

♣ K764

If you place East with the ace it may suit you to lead ♣2 towards the king. If East plays his ace on air, he will have to pay for the privilege – by giving you a third club trick. If instead he plays low, you can switch your attention elsewhere, with one club trick in the bag.

If West holds the missing ace in that club position you can do even better, leading twice towards the queen-jack. The full deal might look like this:

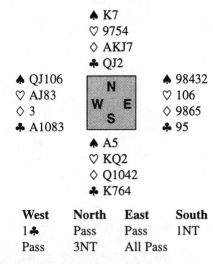

```
                ♠ K7
                ♡ 9754
                ◇ AKJ7
                ♣ QJ2
  ♠ QJ106                   ♠ 98432
  ♡ AJ83      N             ♡ 106
  ◇ 3       W   E           ◇ 9865
  ♣ A1083      S            ♣ 95
                ♠ A5
                ♡ KQ2
                ◇ Q1042
                ♣ K764
```

West	North	East	South
1♣	Pass	Pass	1NT
Pass	3NT	All Pass	

West leads the queen of spades against 3NT. You win with the ace and lead a club towards dummy. If West rises with the ace you will have nine tricks. Suppose instead that he plays low and dummy's queen wins. You return to your hand with ◇ 10 and lead another club. Again West cannot afford to rise with the ace and dummy's jack wins the trick. With two club tricks safely gathered, you can establish your ninth trick in hearts.

One of the prettiest examples of avoidance play is known as the Morton's Fork:

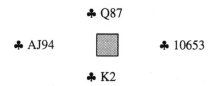

♣ Q87

♣ AJ94   ♣ 10653

♣ K2

Placing West with the ace, you lead ♣2 from the South hand. If West rises, he gives you two club tricks. If he plays low, the queen wins and you may be able to discard your remaining club on a surplus winner in dummy. West loses out either way.

World champion, Sandra Landy, wielded the Morton's Fork on this deal:

Game All. Dealer West.

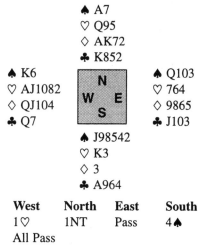

♠ A7
♡ Q95
◇ AK72
♣ K852

♠ K6   ♠ Q103
♡ AJ1082   ♡ 764
◇ QJ104   ◇ 9865
♣ Q7   ♣ J103

♠ J98542
♡ K3
◇ 3
♣ A964

West	North	East	South
1♡	1NT	Pass	4♠
All Pass			

West led the queen of diamonds and it seemed at first glance that declarer would lose two trumps, one heart and one club. However, Landy won the diamond lead, ruffed a diamond in the South hand, then led a low heart. If West had risen with the heart ace, declarer would have had two discards for her club losers; she would lose just one heart and two trumps. West in fact played low, dummy's queen winning the trick. Landy now cashed the ace of trumps and discarded her remaining heart on the king of diamonds. A second round of trumps came next and when the club suit eventually broke 3-2 she had ten tricks.

Suppose, on the above deal, that East had opened the bidding instead of West. Declarer would play the heart suit differently – low towards the king. East would now be caught on the prongs!

11

SEEING THROUGH THE DEFENDERS' CARDS

'Know your customer' is the advice given on training courses for salesmen. The world's top card-players also know their customers. They know what honour combinations they like to lead from, what holdings they are more likely to switch from, how they will react in various situations.

Suppose you are in a suit contract and the opening lead is the jack of an unbid suit? It *might* be from jack doubleton or from a sequence headed by the KJ10. Not very often, though. Nearly always it will be from a J109 or J108 combination. Tony faced such a situation on this deal from the 1994 Lederer Memorial Trophy.

Love All. Dealer North.

```
              ♠ Q1032
              ♡ A94
              ◇ AQ2
              ♣ A86
  ♠ 764                      ♠ AJ85
  ♡ KQ10         N           ♡ J7
  ◇ J1084      W   E         ◇ K965
  ♣ Q32          S           ♣ J107
              ♠ K9
              ♡ 86532
              ◇ 73
              ♣ K954
```

West	North	East	South
Calderwood	*Robson*	*Shek*	*Forrester*
–	1NT	Pass	2♡
Pass	2NT	Pass	3♡
All Pass			

A natural system was being played. North's 1NT showed 14-16 and the Two Hearts response was natural, indicating 0-9 points. North's 2NT showed a flat maximum with heart support. (You would have stopped safely in Two Hearts, we realise!)

When West led ◊J many players would say: it can't cost anything to finesse; West may have led from KJ10. Players rarely lead from such a combination and Tony preferred to rise with dummy's ace. A spade to the king was followed by ♡9, run to East's jack.

East could not cash the ◊K at this stage or he would set up a second discard for declarer's club losers (the other would come from the spade suit). He switched instead to the ♣J, won with the ace. The queen of spades was covered and ruffed. Tony then crossed to the ace of trumps and led the good ♠10, discarding his diamond loser. As it happens, West had to ruff from the three-card trump holding. Tony ruffed the diamond return and played a trump, felling the king and jack. With a spare trump left in dummy, the contract would have made now even if the clubs had broken 4-2.

Success on this deal sprung from declarer's card-reading at trick 1. Had he finessed in diamonds there would have been no recovery.

When a defender does something out of the ordinary, ask yourself 'why did they do that?' Bobby Wolff came up with the right answer on this deal played against France in the 1971 world championship.

Game All. Dealer East.

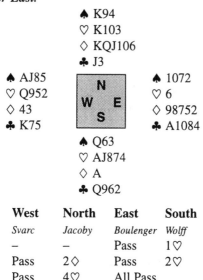

```
              ♠ K94
              ♡ K103
              ◊ KQJ106
              ♣ J3
  ♠ AJ85                    ♠ 1072
  ♡ Q952         N          ♡ 6
  ◊ 43       W       E      ◊ 98752
  ♣ K75          S          ♣ A1084
              ♠ Q63
              ♡ AJ874
              ◊ A
              ♣ Q962
```

West	North	East	South
Svarc	*Jacoby*	*Boulenger*	*Wolff*
–	–	Pass	1♡
Pass	2◊	Pass	2♡
Pass	4♡	All Pass	

West led ♣5 to the ace and won the ♠2 return with the ace. He next cashed the king of clubs and exited with a spade. Does anything strike you as strange about that? By cashing the king of clubs, setting up South's queen for a spade discard from dummy, West made it clear that he was hoping for a setting trick from the trump suit. It seemed to Wolff that West would normally have returned a spade ... unless he had good grounds for expecting the defence to score a trump trick!

Following this hunch, Wolff won the spade switch in his hand and led the trump jack. Svarc covered with the queen and dummy's king won the trick. Wolff now asked himself why West had covered the jack of trumps. From a holding such as Q52 or Q2 it would be poor defence indeed; declarer might be leading the jack from AJ9xx, hoping to tempt a cover. No, West surely held the 9 himself, very likely in a 4-card holding. Wolff returned to his hand with the ace of diamonds and ran the 8 of trumps, finessing successfully against West's 9. It would be hard to beat that as an example of card reading.

On many hands it is not particularly difficult to 'know where the cards are'. Look at this deal from a Scottish pairs event.

Love All. Dealer North.

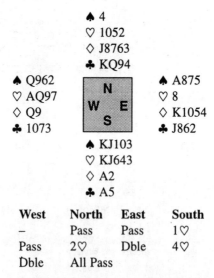

	♠ 4	
	♡ 1052	
	◊ J8763	
	♣ KQ94	

♠ Q962		♠ A875
♡ AQ97		♡ 8
◊ Q9		◊ K1054
♣ 1073		♣ J862

	♠ KJ103	
	♡ KJ643	
	◊ A2	
	♣ A5	

West	North	East	South
–	Pass	Pass	1♡
Pass	2♡	Dble	4♡
Dble	All Pass		

West leads ♠2 to the ace and East (who would have done better to return a trump) switches to ◊4. Declarer has a near perfect picture of the defenders' hands already. With five spades East would surely have bid Two Spades rather than double; the spades are therefore 4-4. In Europe, at least, the lead of a low card proclaims an honour in the suit led. That marks West with four spades to the queen. Similarly, East's ◊ 4 suggests four cards to a single honour; with both honours he would have switched to the king. East's hand will not therefore be a million miles away from:

> ♠ Axxx
> ♡ x
> ◊ Kxxx
> ♣ Jxxx

You win the diamond switch with the ace, cash the king of spades, and lead the spade jack. When West covers, you ruff in the dummy and play three rounds of clubs, discarding a diamond. After ruffing a diamond, you cash ♠ 10. These cards are still out:

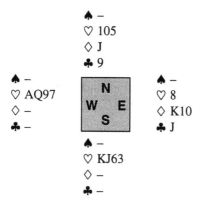

> ♠ –
> ♡ 105
> ◊ J
> ♣ 9

♠ –   ♠ –
♡ AQ97   ♡ 8
◊ –   ◊ K10
♣ –   ♣ J

> ♠ –
> ♡ KJ63
> ◊ –
> ♣ –

You lead a low trump towards the 10 and West is restricted to two trump tricks, whether or not he puts in the queen.

The Principle of Restricted Choice

USA faced Sweden in the semi-finals of the 1992 Olympiad and the Swedes stopped in Six Clubs on the deal below. Bob Hamman carried his side all the way to Seven Clubs and found he had a critical guess to make in the trump suit.

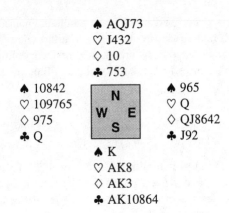

```
                    ♠ AQJ73
                    ♡ J432
                    ◇ 10
                    ♣ 753
   ♠ 10842                         ♠ 965
   ♡ 109765      N                 ♡ Q
   ◇ 975       W     E             ◇ QJ8642
   ♣ Q           S                 ♣ J92
                    ♠ K
                    ♡ AK8
                    ◇ AK3
                    ♣ AK10864
```

Hamman won the spade lead with the king and cashed the ace of trumps, the queen showing from West. He now had to guess whether West had started with QJ doubleton in the trump suit or single queen. What would you say are the relative probabilities of those two holdings?

The original chance of West being dealt ♣QJ is roughly the same as that of being dealt a single ♣Q. But we have not yet taken into account a very important consideration. Holding both the queen and jack, West might have chosen to play the jack instead of the queen. In effect this halves the chance that the queen was a chosen play from QJ. It is roughly *twice as likely* that the queen is a singleton.

One of the world's top professionals, Bob Hamman does not ignore odds like that. He reached dummy with a diamond ruff and took a successful finesse of ♣10, claiming the contract.

(If your schooldays are still fresh in the mind, you may remember this mathematically equivalent problem. A boy has two unmarked bags, one filled with red sweets, the other filled with an even mixture of red and green sweets. He chooses a bag at random, puts his hand in, and pulls out a red sweet. Which bag did he choose? Once again, it is *twice as likely* that he chose the bag containing only red sweets.)

Some bridge players will argue the point endlessly. If you're not convinced, look at it another way. Roughly speaking, these three situations are equally likely:

West was dealt ♣QJ
West was dealt ♣Q
West was dealt ♣J

So, if you read West for a singleton when he plays either the queen or the jack, you will win twice as often as you lose. And those figures hold good whatever strategy West uses to choose a card from QJ doubleton. This concept is known as …

The Principle of Restricted Choice
It is more likely that a defender played a card because he
had no choice than that he chose to play it from equals.

There are many everyday situations where it will guide you to the best play. Suppose you can afford only one loser from this suit:

♡ Q764

♡ A932

You cash the ace and the 10 appears from East. What now? You should duck the next round, playing East for K10 rather than J10. As before, the odds are nearly 2-1 in favour of this play. The same would apply if East had played the jack on the first round, of course. You win against KJ and K10, pay out only to J10.

♡ K972

♡ AQ5

Here you cash the ace and queen, East dropping the jack (or 10) on the second round. Again the odds strongly favour a finesse on the third round. There are many such situations.

When a defender may have had to make a choice from three equal cards, the principle applies with even greater force.

♣ K53

♣ AQ82

You cash the ace and king, West dropping the 9 and jack. When you lead a third round East produces the last remaining small card. Only the 10 is out. Should you finesse or not? You probably feel that it is right to finesse. It is indeed, and the odds in favour of this play are no less than 3-1! The odds of West having been dealt ♣J9 are three times as great as him having chosen to play that particular pair of cards from ♣J109.

Clues from the auction

When the opponents have been in the auction it is often possible to read the position of the high cards as early as trick 1. This deal arose in a 1995 Premier League match between the teams of Hackett and Tredinnick.

Tony was sitting in his favourite 'South' seat.

North/South Game. Dealer East.

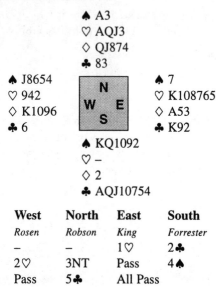

```
                    ♠ A3
                    ♡ AQJ3
                    ◇ QJ874
                    ♣ 83
        ♠ J8654                   ♠ 7
        ♡ 942            N         ♡ K108765
        ◇ K1096       W   E       ◇ A53
        ♣ 6             S         ♣ K92
                    ♠ KQ1092
                    ♡ –
                    ◇ 2
                    ♣ AQJ10754
```

West	North	East	South
Rosen	*Robson*	*King*	*Forrester*
–	–	1♡	2♣
2♡	3NT	Pass	4♠
Pass	5♣	All Pass	

West led ◇10, covered by the queen and ace, and East returned a low diamond. On the play so far, you can place West with the diamond king. To make up his opening bid, East must surely hold the king of hearts and the king of clubs. So, you start by ruffing the diamond return, crossing to the ace of spades, and finessing in trumps. Right? That's how most players would tackle the hand. With the trump king still guarded, it would then require an inspired view in the spade suit to make the contract.

Instead, Tony considered what the position would be if he played the ace and queen of trumps from his hand. He would then have ten top tricks – six trumps, three spades and the heart ace. The position of the red kings was known and it followed that neither defender would be able to retain four spades when the trump suit was run. If West held four or more spades he would be squeezed in spades and diamonds. If East held the spade length, he would be squeezed in the majors.

Fortified by this analysis, Tony played the ace of trumps followed by the queen. East won and returned a diamond, ruffed in the South hand. When trumps were run, this end position developed:

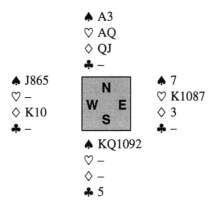

♠ A3
♡ AQ
◇ QJ
♣ –

♠ J865   ♠ 7
♡ –   ♡ K1087
◇ K10   ◇ 3
♣ –   ♣ –

♠ KQ1092
♡ –
◇ –
♣ 5

West could afford a diamond on the last trump, but had no good discard when Tony crossed to the spade ace and cashed the ace of hearts. Interesting, isn't it, that this ending (a single squeeze, played as a double squeeze) could be predicted with some certainty after the first trick?

Opening bids that show a weak two-suiter are becoming increasingly popular. They absorb bidding space, it's true, but there is a price to be paid when the other side buys the contract. Declarer will have a near perfect picture of the defenders' distribution right from the start. Andy Robson was off to a flying start, after such an opening, on this deal from a match between Great Britain and Iceland.

Love All. Dealer West.

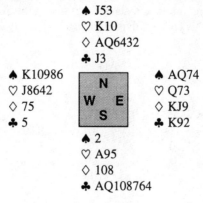

```
                    ♠ J53
                    ♡ K10
                    ◇ AQ6432
                    ♣ J3
  ♠ K10986                         ♠ AQ74
  ♡ J8642          N               ♡ Q73
  ◇ 75         W       E           ◇ KJ9
  ♣ 5              S               ♣ K92
                    ♠ 2
                    ♡ A95
                    ◇ 108
                    ♣ AQ108764
```

West	North	East	South
	Forrester		*Robson*
2◇	3◇	4♠	5♣
Pass	Pass	Dble	All Pass

West's opening bid showed a weak two-suiter in the majors. Since North-South held nine clubs between them and only eight diamonds, it was already a fair bet that West held 5-5-2-1 shape rather than 5-5-1-2. This proposition was bolstered by East's final double.

Two rounds of spades were played, Robson ruffing the second round. You can see the problem he faced. If he used one of dummy's trumps to ruff his heart loser, it would no longer be possible to pick up East's king of trumps.

Relying on his inferred count of the hand, Robson ran ◇ 10 at trick two, losing to the jack. A low heart was returned, giving declarer the chance to play for split honours in the suit. Robson showed that it was not necessary to rely on this. He won with the ace and crossed to the ace of diamonds, both defenders following. He then called for the jack of trumps. If East were to cover, declarer would win with the ace, ruff the heart loser, and claim. East in fact held off his king of trumps, leaving the lead in dummy. Robson ruffed the diamonds good, returned to dummy with the king of hearts, and led a master diamond. It was the end of the road for East. If he ruffed, declarer would overruff, ruff his heart loser, and later draw the bare king of trumps with the ace. If instead East discarded, declarer would throw his heart loser and repeat the trump finesse.

Believe the defenders' cards

Should you pay close attention to the spot-cards the defenders play? Or are they out to catch you? Declarer on the following deal was unwilling to believe the defenders' cards and talked himself into going one down.

Game All. Dealer South.

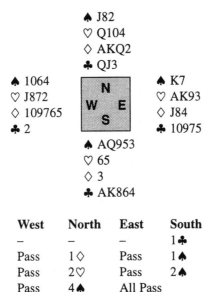

```
              ♠ J82
              ♡ Q104
              ◇ AKQ2
              ♣ QJ3
  ♠ 1064                      ♠ K7
  ♡ J872         N            ♡ AK93
  ◇ 109765    W     E         ◇ J84
  ♣ 2            S            ♣ 10975
              ♠ AQ953
              ♡ 65
              ◇ 3
              ♣ AK864
```

West	North	East	South
–	–	–	1♣
Pass	1◇	Pass	1♠
Pass	2♡	Pass	2♠
Pass	4♠	All Pass	

West led ♡2 against Four Spades, East winning dummy's 10 with the king and cashing the ace of hearts. The ♣10 switch was won in the dummy and declarer continued with a trump to the queen, winning the trick. There was no problem if trumps were 3-2. What if East held ♠K10xx?

Declarer thought he saw the answer. On the second round of trumps he led low to dummy's jack. Had West shown out, East winning with the king, declarer could have picked up East's remaining 10x. What in fact happened was that East won with the trump king and gave his partner a club ruff. One down!

There are two points worthy of note. Firstly, the vast majority of defenders play their low spot-cards in the trump suit from the bottom. So, from K1076 they play the 6. In theory they should no doubt choose randomly, but in practice very few do. Since it was therefore unlikely that East held K1076, it was not worth taking any substantial risk to pick up such a holding. More importantly, there was a better safety play available anyway. After winning the spade queen, declarer should have crossed to the ace of diamonds and led the 8 of trumps, planning to run it if East produced the 6. The king would have made a welcome appearance, giving declarer eleven tricks instead of nine.

Pursuing our theme of believing the defenders' cards, see what you make of this 3NT played by Tony at a critical stage of the 1993 Gold Cup quarter-final between Kirby and Chambers. (We don't have the space to explain why ... but Tony's team was 65 IMPs down at half-time. This deal began a successful recovery.)

North/South Game. Dealer North.

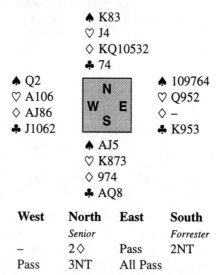

```
               ♠ K83
               ♡ J4
               ◇ KQ10532
               ♣ 74
  ♠ Q2            N          ♠ 109764
  ♡ A106       W     E       ♡ Q952
  ◇ AJ86          S          ◇ –
  ♣ J1062                    ♣ K953
               ♠ AJ5
               ♡ K873
               ◇ 974
               ♣ AQ8
```

West	North	East	South
	Senior		*Forrester*
–	2◇	Pass	2NT
Pass	3NT	All Pass	

The opening bid was a Weak Two in diamonds, with Tony's 2NT an enquiry bid. North's 3NT response showed a maximum with two of the top three diamond honours and this became the final contract. West led ♣2 to his partner's king, declarer winning with the ace. A diamond was led to the king, East showing out on the trick. The declarers at both tables reached this point. How would you have continued?

Realising that two entries were needed to the South hand, in order to pick up the diamonds, the other declarer banked his hopes on a finesse of the spade jack. Unlucky. West won with the queen and the game went one down.

Tony preferred to rely on West's ♣2 lead, proclaiming a 4-card suit. He crossed to the spade ace and led ◇9, covered by the jack and queen. Now came a club to the queen, baring the defences in that suit, followed by another diamond. West scored ♣J10 and the two red aces, but declarer had the balance. (In a perfect world the defenders would still have beaten the contract. West would unblock ♣10 under the queen and later play jack and another club to partner's 9. This would squeeze the dummy to a blank ♡J and East could then play ♡Q through.)

What should your reaction be when a defender signals that he has a strong holding in a suit? Should you immediately conclude that a key finesse is not working or do you think it's a bluff? Our advice is that you will gain much more by believing such signals than by assuming that the defenders are up to mischief. Look at this deal, played by Cliff Yang of the USA:

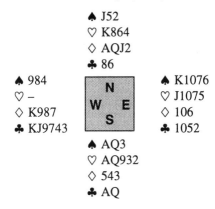

```
              ♠ J52
              ♡ K864
              ◇ AQJ2
              ♣ 86
  ♠ 984                   ♠ K1076
  ♡ –          N          ♡ J1075
  ◇ K987    W     E       ◇ 106
  ♣ KJ9743     S          ♣ 1052
              ♠ AQ3
              ♡ AQ932
              ◇ 543
              ♣ AQ
```

Yang ended in Six Hearts and West led ♠9, won with the queen. To cash the ace of trumps now would cost the contract; declarer would no longer be able to catch East's trump holding. Realising that he could cope with a 4-0 break only if East held the four trumps, declarer continued accurately with a trump to king. He then played a trump to the 9, East not splitting his honours. Meanwhile, West had not been sitting idly. He had thrown the 9 and 3 of clubs, showing something good in that suit. Yang took a successful diamond finesse, then drew East's remaining trumps. How should declarer continue, do you think? Should he repeat the diamond finesse and test for a 3-3 break in that suit, falling back on the club finesse if necessary? That line would lead to defeat.

After West's emphatic signal in clubs declarer rejected any line which might involve a club finesse. Instead he exited with ace and another spade, rectifying the count for a squeeze. When East won and switched to a club, declarer rose with the ace. These cards remained:

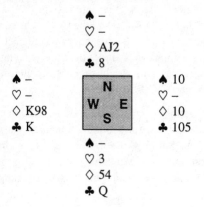

West had no card to spare on the last trump. When he chose to throw a diamond, declarer repeated the diamond finesse and claimed the last two tricks with the ace and 2 of diamonds. Of course it was a poor idea for West to signal his holding in clubs. What use could such a signal be to his partner?

Zia Mahmood once contributed a valuable Bols Bridge Tip: if a defender does not cover, he does not hold the missing honour. Tony had the tip in mind when, partnered by Ian Monachan, he tackled this deal from a Swiss Teams event in London:

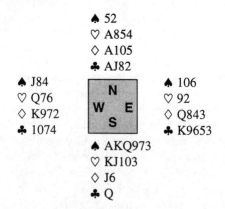

West found the best attack against South's Six Hearts, leading ◇2. Tony won with the ace, crossed to the spade ace, and led ♣Q. When West played low, it was a reasonable assumption that East held the king. (Again, do not say to yourself 'West is a good player. He's quite clever enough to hold off the king.' In practice, defenders do not make such plays; there is rarely any way for them to know it will be good defence.)

Tony overtook ♣Q with dummy's ace and played ace and another trump, East following with the 2 and the 9. The percentage play in the trump suit alone, is to finesse the queen. But a losing finesse would cost the contract, since West would cash a diamond trick. Tony preferred to put up the king of trumps. The queen refused to drop, West following with a small card. When Tony turned to the spade suit, luck finally came his way. West, who held the master trump, had to follow three times. Two diamonds were thrown from dummy on the third and fourth rounds of spades; the trump queen was the only trick for the defence.

Tony had combined three different chances. The first was that the club king might be onside (rejected when West did not cover). The second was that the queen of trumps might fall doubleton. The final chance was that the defender with the trump queen would also hold three spades, allowing dummy's diamonds to be thrown in time.

Is there such a thing as a consistently lucky player? Not in terms of the number of aces and kings that a player is dealt, but there are certainly those who make the most of any luck that comes their way. That notoriously poor card holder, A. R. Forrester, sat South on this deal from the 1987 Bermuda Bowl round-robin:

East/West Game. Dealer East.

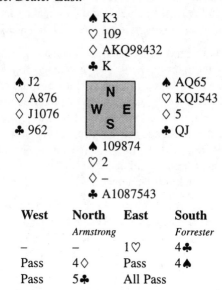

```
                    ♠ K3
                    ♡ 109
                    ◇ AKQ98432
                    ♣ K
   ♠ J2                              ♠ AQ65
   ♡ A876            N               ♡ KQJ543
   ◇ J1076       W       E           ◇ 5
   ♣ 962             S               ♣ QJ
                    ♠ 109874
                    ♡ 2
                    ◇ -
                    ♣ A1087543
```

West	North	East	South
	Armstrong		*Forrester*
–	–	1♡	4♣
Pass	4◇	Pass	4♠
Pass	5♣	All Pass	

South should perhaps have passed 4◇. Still, it's difficult to let partner choose trumps when you have such a *powerful* two-suiter.

West led a trump, not the most effective attack, and the East's jack fell under the dummy's king. The heart loser was spirited away on ◇A and declarer crossed to his hand with a heart ruff. (Had he carelessly attempted a diamond ruff instead, East would have ruffed with his remaining honour, promoting West's 9 of trumps.) The ace of trumps dropped East's queen and Tony drew West's last trump with the 10.

Declarer could afford only two spade losers. One obvious chance was that West held three spades to the ace. How likely was that, though? The defenders held 21 points between them. East, who had opened the bidding, figured to hold between 12 and 19 points, West between 1 and 8. On those numbers alone, East was a strong favourite to hold the spade ace. For what it was worth, also, East had produced the king on the first round of hearts. This *might* be a non-standard card but most defenders play the ace from ace-king when following in the second seat. And if West did hold ♡A, he could hardly hold another ace and not double the final contract.

Tony led ♠10, intending to run it. Whether or not this card was covered, he would now escape with only two spade losers. As you see, even unlucky card holders do occasionally have fortune turning their way!